# THE ROAD
# TO FINANCIAL
# REFORMATION

# THE ROAD TO FINANCIAL REFORMATION

*Warnings, Consequences, Reforms*

## HENRY KAUFMAN

WILEY

JOHN WILEY & SONS, INC.

Published by John Wiley & Sons, Inc., Hoboken, New Jersey.
Published simultaneously in Canada.

For general information on our other products and services or for technical support, please contact our Customer Care Department within the United States at (800) 762-2974, outside the United States at (317) 572-3993 or fax (317) 572-4002.

Wiley also publishes its books in a variety of electronic formats. Some content that appears in print may not be available in electronic books. For more information about Wiley products, visit our web site at www.wiley.com.

*Library of Congress Cataloging-in-Publication Data:*

Kaufman, Henry.

The road to financial reformation: warnings, consequences, reforms / Henry Kaufman.
    p.   cm.
Includes bibliographical references and index.
ISBN 978-0-470-53212-6 (cloth)
    1. Finance–Government policy.   2. International finance–Government policy.   I. Title.
HG173.K3644
2009 332—dc22

2009017157

Printed in the United States of America.
10 9 8 7 6 5 4 3 2 1

To
Helen Katcher
for her invaluable support of my career

The boast of heraldry, the pomp of pow'r,

And all that beauty, all that wealth e'er gave,

Awaits alike th' inevitable hour.

The paths of glory lead but to the grave.

Ninth stanza of "Elegy Written in a Country Churchyard" by Thomas Gray (1716–1771)

# Contents

## PART IV: FINANCIAL CRISES

## PART V: POLICY FAILURES AND REFORMS

## PART VI: PROSPECTS

# *Foreword*

I first met Henry Kaufman in 2001. We were in New York and I had just
given some lectures at New York University's Stern School of Business.
At Oxford University, where I was still based at that time, the buildings are mostly named after long-dead prelates. As a freshman undergraduate, I had a bedroom in the Waynflete Building, which commemorated a
bishop who died in 1486. New York University is not like that. I had
just given a lecture in the Kaufman Management Center—and here was
the eponymous benefactor himself, sitting on the other side of the lunch
table, very much alive.

"Niall," he said, coming directly to the point, "your books all seem
to be concerned with money and power."

I could not deny it.

"So," he continued, "why don't you come to where the money and
the power actually *are*?"

Not long after that, I resigned my Oxford professorship and accepted
a job at NYU. With that clarity I have come to see as his defining char-
acteristic, Henry had posed a question to which there could be only
one answer. If I really wanted to be serious about financial history, I was
wasting my time in buildings named after bishops.

Henry Kaufman is living financial history. A refugee from Hitler's
Germany, he studied economics and finance at NYU and Columbia
before joining the Federal Reserve Bank of New York as an economist in 1957. Five years later he moved to Salomon Brothers, where
he spent more than a quarter of a century as head of research and later
vice-chairman. Like my NYU colleague Nouriel Roubini, he earned

the soubriquet "Dr. Doom," in his case for consistently (and correctly) warning that the inflation of the 1970s would drive up long-term interest rates. When he called the bottom of the bond market in 1982, it was the beginning of what George Soros has called a 25-year "super bubble," as interest rates came steadily back down and asset prices took off.

"My generation," Kaufman recently remarked in an interview, "is imbued with a greater fear of risk that just wasn't evident in our current leaders." That may explain why, throughout the period from 1982 until 2007, he never succumbed to the irrational exuberance that afflicted so many other investors, bankers, and fund managers. On the contrary, as this fascinating volume shows, he presciently warned of the systemic vulnerabilities that were accumulating in the American financial system.

In particular, he warned time and again of the dangers inherent in the rise of very large financial conglomerates such as Citigroup and Bank of America. He staunchly opposed the repeal of the 1933 Glass-Steagall Act, which had separated commercial and investment banking in the wake of the Depression. He expressed anxiety, too, about the excessive concentration of commercial bank deposits and mutual funds, and about the merging under one corporate roof of financial activities as diverse as deposit taking, insurance, leasing, securities trading, asset management, consumer finance, and credit card lending. The evidence he presents here of financial concentration is indeed remarkable. Between 1990 and 2008, the share of financial assets held by the 10 largest U.S. financial institutions rose from 10 percent to 50 percent, even as the number of banks fell from over 15,000 to around 8,000.

But it was not just the scale and scope of financial institutions that changed in the past two decades. The growth of securitization of mortgages and other consumer debt (pioneered by Salomon Brothers in the 1980s), the explosion of derivatives traded on exchanges or sold over the counter, the doubling of turnover on the stock market, and, above all, the vast increase of leverage on bank balance sheets—all these changes were correctly identified by Kaufman as increasing the risk of a crisis.

Contrary to the conventional wisdom of the time, which maintained that risk was being optimally distributed to "those best able to bear it," he saw that it was in fact becoming suboptimally concentrated on (and off) the balance sheets of around 15 institutions. By the end of 2007, these institutions, with combined shareholder equity of $857 billion, had total assets of $13.6 trillion and off-balance-sheet commitments of $5.8 trillion—a leverage ratio of 23 to 1. They also had underwritten derivatives with a gross notional value of $216 trillion.

Even as he was pointing out the dangers of these trends in the marketplace, Kaufman was also expressing concern about defects of U.S. monetary policy. In 2002, for example, he questioned the then Federal Reserve Chairman Alan Greenspan's assertion that it was almost beyond the capability of a central bank to "identify a bubble in the process of inflating." Indeed, he realized early on that Greenspan's "monetary gradualism" was one of the *causes* of the successive bubbles in the stock market and the real estate market.

In addition, Kaufman regularly voiced his unease about the inadequacy of financial regulation. As early as 1985 he called for a National Board of Overseers of Financial Institutions and Markets, with a counterpart entity operating at the international level. It is a call he repeats here, arguing that a Federal Financial Oversight authority should take over from the private rating agencies the role of rating the credit of institutions and financial instruments. It remains to be seen if the new unitary regulator envisaged by Treasury Secretary Timothy Geithner will be entrusted with this task.

Perhaps the most important theme that runs through this book, however, is the importance of financial history. Because the structure of financial markets is constantly changing as a result of innovation and regulatory change, Kaufman argues, it is potentially fatal to base investment decisions on mathematical models feeding off relatively short runs of data. (Typically, value-at-risk models calculate a firm's potential exposure to losses using just three years of data, and sometimes even less.) Far more valuable is the historical approach, which—as Kaufman so ably demonstrates—allows us to envisage more than the possible future on the basis of analogies with the past. (Read his chapter on the credit crunch of 1966 for further evidence that—as Mark Twain said—while history never repeats itself, it certainly rhymes.) In Kaufman's words, "Amid the blizzard of quantitative, technical offerings ... courses in economic and financial history should be required for all business degrees." Amen to that.

With the benefit of hindsight, future historians will doubtless agree with Henry Kaufman about the roles of banking concentration, financial innovation, monetary laxity, and defective regulation in causing the 2007–2009 crisis. The difference is that he saw the potentially lethal consequences *before* disaster struck. At the time, unfortunately, most people paid too little heed to his warnings. With the publication of *The Road to Financial Reformation*, we have a chance to pay a great deal more attention to the remedies and reforms Henry Kaufman now proposes.

NIALL FERGUSON
William Ziegler Professor of Business Administration
Harvard Business School
Author of *The Ascent of Money*

# Acknowledgments

As with my previous book, *On Money and Markets*, David Sicilia, a business and economic historian at the University of Maryland, played an indispensible editorial role in helping shape the content and prose of this project as well. His ongoing advice made the writing of this book less solitary and more fulfilling, and for that I am very grateful.

At Henry Kaufman & Company, Helen Katcher—somehow having survived more than four decades in my employ—demonstrated yet again her apparently bottomless patience as she assembled documents, collated drafts, and otherwise allowed this project to intrude on her other duties. Peter Rup demonstrated wizardry in culling data for most of the figures in this book from various financial databases.

Countless other Wall Street colleagues contributed to my thinking for this book in large and small ways. At the risk of offending many others through failure of omission, let me give several honorable mentions. Two former colleagues from my many years at Salomon Brothers—Thomas Klaffky and Richard Berner—supplied me with useful data on credit and debt. And as they have as friends and associates for decades, Robert DiClemente, Marty Leibowitz, Mickey Levy, John Lipsky, John Makin, Leonard Santow, Nick Sargen, Kim Schoenholtz, Paul Volcker, and Al Wojnilower stimulated and challenged my thinking about finance and the economy.

At John Wiley & Sons, Pamela van Giessen saw the promise in this project from the start, and ushered it through with a firm and intelligent editorial hand.

# *Introduction*

Financial crises are deeply embedded in my early childhood memories. Although I was born a few years after the hyperinflation of the early 1920s in Germany, my family had endured that punishing event. Hyperinflation left an indelible scar on my then middle-aged grandfather. Unable to forget the hardships and financial losses of the tumultuous period, he spoke of them often—of the loans he extended to farmers that were repaid with bushels of worthless money, the food shortages created when prices of some commodities rose faster than money could be printed, the suffering that families endured when their hard-earned savings evaporated, the widespread anxiety in a society with a collapsing economy.

Although my father never spoke of those grim years, I knew he was deeply troubled by the aftershocks of the German hyperinflation, especially the rise of Hitler. He correctly sensed that Nazism would threaten our very existence. At the dinner table, conversation often turned to the subject of whether we should leave Germany. My father urged the move, but my grandparents, whose ancestral roots in the country extended back hundreds of years, resisted. The debate was settled during an evening of terror in January 1937, when members of a Nazi torchlight parade ransacked our home.

It took my family most of that year to make our way safely to the United States. Having fled one crisis, we arrived on the heels of another—the Great Depression. Although elated to reach the safety of American shores, we nevertheless faced daunting economic prospects. Our savings were modest, and jobs were still scarce during the decade's second slump, the so-called Roosevelt Recession of 1937–1938. But my father eventually found work—a six-day-a-week job in a meatpacking plant that paid 25 cents an hour. Meanwhile, my mother, who had never worked outside our home, became a house cleaner to help make ends meet, leaving me in the care of my grandparents. The worst depression in modern history lingered on.

In ways difficult to measure, these formative experiences surely influenced my views as I built a career in financial markets. Over the years I thought a lot about the interplay between economic and financial activity, about financial market behavior, and about structural changes in the financial markets and their implications for official policies. I ultimately reached the conclusion that financial institutions play a crucial and special role in our society; they are not the same as completely private-sector firms such as chemical companies or department stores. Their role is so pervasive and indispensable that they require close public scrutiny.

One reason financial institutions must be especially vigilant to act responsibly is that their capital base is quite small relative to their assets and liabilities, which consist of temporary funds and deposits of households, firms, and governments. They finance a variety of demanders of credit. When they perform this role as intermediaries well, our economy and society benefit. When they don't, our economy and financial markets suffer, and, in extreme cases, crises may follow. Financial institutions therefore need to balance their entrepreneurial drive with their fiduciary responsibility.

In most cases when this balance is not maintained, it is because entrepreneurial risk taking wins out. Because financial institutions are highly leveraged, incremental increases in leverage and in other forms of risk taking—although they may boost near-term profits—can lead to liquidity problems and even solvency problems, both for the institution and for its clients. And when entrepreneurial risk taking becomes pervasive throughout financial markets, a financial crisis can take hold. What concerns me most about credit crises is the potential risk they pose to our society. Extreme crises can cause political upheaval, as they did in the Germany of my childhood. Short of that, a serious financial crisis still holds the potential of transforming our society from an imperfect economic democracy into a socialist system.

Dangers that grave were not on the immediate horizon during my early days in the financial markets in the 1950s. The financial legislation of the 1930s had put in place constraints on financial practices and had defined the boundaries within which major financial institutions such as commercial and investment banks could operate. More than that, many of the managers of leading financial institutions still wore the scars of the Great Depression. They were not about to repeat the reckless financial practices that preceded those woeful years, nor were many of their children, who also refrained from highly speculative market behavior.

But the financial restraint of the postwar environment began to change one almost imperceptible step at a time. In the early 1960s, the Federal Reserve began to allow commercial banks to issue large-denominated negotiable certificates of deposit (CDs) up to an imposed interest rate ceiling. In this limited way, banks were allowed to participate in markets as bidders for funds. Although this measure hardly seemed monumental at the time, it proved to be the opening wedge for other forms of regulatory liberalization. At the time, Fed officials simply did not recognize the implications the new CD policy held for the realignment of markets, nor were they concerned when new credit instruments were introduced soon thereafter.

Within a few years, increased competition in commercial banking resulted in the first credit crisis in the post–World War II period—the credit crunch of 1966. Even though deposit rates reached the Fed's imposed ceilings, money rates climbed above them. My recollection of this event, which I describe later in this book, is that it caused a brief but intense period of anxiety in the markets. It was followed by 14 other credit crises. In each case, deteriorating credit quality was associated with liberal lending and investing practices.

Even so, credit markets continued to expand rapidly. Many new credit instruments and trading practices appeared on the scene, and financial markets became thoroughly global. The balance tipped more and more toward entrepreneurial risk taking. Securitization, especially the increasing use of derivatives, proved to be an enticing elixir for middle managers at financial institutions in search of near-term profits. Those rewards translated into generous bonuses. For their part, some senior managers at financial firms applauded risk taking that increased earnings per share, option grants, and other measures of success.

By the 1980s, I was quite concerned not only about how structural changes in the financial markets were encouraging excessive risk taking, but also about the failure of government officials in the Federal Reserve and elsewhere to change how they supervised financial markets accordingly. I expressed these concerns in several papers I presented at the Jackson Hole conferences in Wyoming, sponsored by the Federal Reserve Bank of Kansas City. Then, as now, the Jackson Hole meetings attracted senior central bankers from the United States and abroad, as well as leading economists and government officials. In a paper I delivered on two separate occasions, I described at length many structural changes in the financial markets, and called for the Federal Reserve and other regulatory authorities to incorporate these changes into monetary policies and financial supervision. But my warnings went unheeded, as did my recommendations, which I have developed in greater detail since. At the heart of those recommendations was the creation of a board of overseers that would centralize the supervision of financial markets. I also proposed that the Federal Reserve give much higher priority to financial oversight in its deliberations.

What happened instead was that the Federal Reserve and other regulatory officials—under the sway of the prevailing free-market ideology—continued to deregulate financial markets and took no real actions to rein in speculative behavior or the dangerously rising tide of securitized debt. Many of the new financial instruments fell outside the purview of official regulation as it had been designed before the securitization revolution, and officials seemed content to keep it that way.

I also called attention in the late 1980s to the deterioration of credit quality of corporate finance in a talk before the National Press Club in Washington, D.C. I had noticed that credit ratings on corporate debt had been eroding badly, and not only because Michael Milken at Drexel Burnham Lambert popularized corporate junk bonds. A growing number of chief financial officers were advocating aggressive financial practices. Corporate failures were still relatively rare, and these CFOs made optimistic cash flow forecasts that tolerated a higher debt load. I believed back then and continued to hold the view right up to the current financial debacle that as the volume of below-investment-grade obligations outpaces investment-grade obligations, financing costs for the weaker securities will rise dramatically during periods of credit restraint. The current crisis is providing ample proof of this observation. And, unfortunately, the full consequences of the problem have not yet been realized.

Another important change in financial markets that I began to warn about has been the rapid increase in financial concentration. Nearly every financial crisis since the Second World War has brought about increased pressures to consolidate. In most cases, smaller and medium-size institutions were absorbed by larger ones. But the trend accelerated dramatically in the late 1980s and the 1990s, as commerce and banking were allowed to merge, and as the firewall separating commercial and investment banking—in place since passage of the Glass-Steagall Act of 1933—was dismantled. In congressional testimony, I opposed both of these landmark steps for a variety of reasons (see Chapters 10 and 11). But the barriers fell, and soon thereafter many business corporations organized financial subsidiaries. Again, neither the monetary officials nor other official supervisory authorities put in place safeguards designed to limit the kinds of abuses that would likely accompany this further liberalization of markets. The current financial crisis owes much of its intensity to that unfettered liberalization.

Although the *economic* impact of the current crisis thankfully has not approached the dimensions of the Great Depression, its *financial* developments and their consequences are approaching those of the 1930s. That raises the question: Why are we so poor at managing our key economic institutions while at the same time so accomplished in medicine, engineering, and telecommunications? Why can we land men on the moon with pinpoint accuracy, yet fail to steer our economy away from the rocks? Why do our computers work so well except when we use them to manage credit risks and to guide monetary policy? The answer lies in methodology. In science and technology, we rely on the scientific method: experimental design with dependent and independent variables and with reproducible results.

Economists and financial experts like to fancy themselves as exact scientists as well. Back in the 1960s, when we landed men on the moon, economists emulated the terminology of space-age navigation. They spoke of "midcourse corrections" and of bringing in the economy for a "soft landing." Since then, quantification and modeling have only grown thicker in the economic profession, where econometricians and other so-called quants employ complicated analytical techniques and mathematical formulas. By the 1980s, many economists had embraced the theory of rational expectations, which essentially held that markets were all-knowing and infallible. All of this infused the profession with an aura of authority, authenticity, and accuracy.

The computations were correct, but far too often the conclusions drawn from them were not. This is because the models rely on historical data but fail to take into account the profound impact of structural changes in our economy and in financial markets that have unfolded in the postwar decades.

Along with economists enamored with their own techniques, credit rating agencies and, as noted, senior managers at many leading financial institutions have contributed to the present financial crisis. But these and other private-sector actors can be faulted only up to a point for their aggressive pursuit of profit. Official supervisors are more culpable for the current market turmoil. As I explain in the book's final section, monetary authorities have pursued anachronistic policies that failed to incorporate structural and behavioral changes in financial markets. For decades, the Federal Reserve has tilted toward the stance that markets would discipline transgressors—a strategy that failed to recognize the risks posed to markets and the economy from the failure of large financial conglomerates.

During the financial crises of the early postwar decades, regulators imposed few if any effective constraints on financial markets. And both the economy and financial markets rebounded quickly. Unfortunately, that is far from likely this time around. The damage is too great. A tidal wave of financial excesses has overwhelmed our markets and our economy. There is no quick fix. Expectations for solvency, profits, and growth are suffering severe retrenchment. The collapse that began in 2007 will affect investor behavior for years to come. Political leaders need to act boldly while ensuring that our market-based economy is not undermined. The financial world looks much different now than it did in the 1930s, so we need a new set of rules and regulations so that our financial institutions balance their entrepreneurial drive with their fiduciary responsibilities.

# PART I
# IN PERSPECTIVE

# 1

# Past Blunders and
# Future Choices

In March 1988, less than six months after the stock market crash of 1987, I extolled the value of financial history to an audience at the New York University Graduate School of Business Administration, and reviewed the key linkages between the explosion of debt and the financial crisis. It would seem pedestrian to exclaim now, 20 years later, that the more things change, the more they stay the same. In 1988, there were too few financial historians, yet the need for them was great (and more so today). Consider the many financial mishaps, abuses, and official policy mistakes that might have been avoided if our financial managers and leaders had gained from these scholars a well-rounded historical financial perspective.

The need for such a perspective was great in 1988 and remains so. Our financial structure both in the United States and abroad continued to change radically. The willingness to take risks remained high, while credit quality deteriorated. Indeed, we were not terribly clear about what we really wanted from our financial system then (a situation that worsened in the intervening 20 years), and how and to whom it was to be held accountable. The occasional stringencies, extreme volatility, and abuses in our financial markets consumed our attention and some-times induced official inquiries—such as the Brady Report of 1987.

3

Prior to becoming U.S. Treasury secretary in 1988, Nicholas F. Brady chaired the Presidential Task Force on Market Mechanisms, which was charged with looking into the causes of the 1987 stock market crash. By and large, however, little was—and continues to be—done through constructive policy changes.

I reminded the audience that financial change was continuing at an extraordinary pace, leaving in its wake opportunities that many sought and high risks that few chose to acknowledge, with the main antidote (at least within the first six months after that crash) from the academic and business worlds a call to teach business ethics. This was not enough then (nor is it enough now). Attempts to deregulate morality have long been part of man's struggle against evil. Ethics and morality are forged in our early upbringing and can, at best, be rekindled at a university, while the lessons of financial history can be fully grasped only with further study.

Many of the distinguishing features of financial life in the twentieth century had historical counterparts. For example, the difficulties our financial institutions experienced periodically with their loans to developing countries such as Mexico, Argentina, and Brazil over the past three decades hardly are unprecedented. International debt had been a recurring problem. Financial history is full of moratoriums, defaults, and confiscations—even though some took false comfort that their loans were safe because sovereign powers, in contrast to business corporations, cannot disappear through insolvency.

A few illustrations over many centuries should make the point clear. In the fourteenth century, when Florence was the world's key banking center, the two leading banking houses collapsed because they had extended too much credit to Edward I, Edward II, and Robert Anjou, King of Naples. The lenders never could get at the collateral that was to secure the loan. As Professor Benjamin Cohen related in his book on this incident, *In Whose Interest? International Banking and American Foreign*

*Policy* (New Haven, CT: Yale University Press, 1986), "Instead of being repaid, the lender was willy-nilly forced to lend more and more and to throw good money after bad in the hope of saving what he had already lent." When England pioneered new horizons in international finance in the nineteenth century, many initial successes were followed by debt problems. There were widespread losses and defaults during the numerous crises in that century involving countries and financial institutions. For example, Baring Brothers, one of the most famous British banking houses, had to be bailed out by the Bank of England and by other institutions when it overextended itself to a weakening Argentina in 1890. All this did not change much in the early part of the twentieth century. Nearly $12 billion of foreign bonds was floated in the United States between 1920 and 1931—a huge sum by the standards of that time—but by 1935, nearly 40 percent of the value of the foreign bonds listed on the New York Stock Exchange was in arrears.

The excessive use of leverage, an ongoing theme throughout financial history, contributed to the failure of 14 railroads during just one panic and to the collapse of 600 banks in another panic during the nineteenth century. The immediate predecessor to the wave of leveraged buyouts and high-risk debt financing that swept the U.S. markets in the 1980s was probably the activities of public utility holding companies in the 1920s. Many of these holding companies financed the acquisitions of independent operating units through the excessive use of debt. When financial problems surfaced for these companies, they were often caused by their subsidiaries' going into arrears on their preferred stock dividends and eliminating their common stock dividends. This choked off all the cash flow to the holding companies, which, in turn, had their own heavy debt burdens and preferred stock dividends to meet.

In their heyday, the public utility holding companies employed new financing techniques with the same zeal that the corporate issuers began to embrace in the 1980s, then just beginning to be known as innovative financing or financial engineering. The techniques employed back in olden times to secure legal control over operating companies included the following: (1) the issuance of a huge volume of bonds; (2) the issuance of nonvoting preferred stock; (3) the issuance of different classes of common stock, with only one having the controlling voting power; (4) the establishment of voting trusts with the shares in the hands of a few voting trustees; and (5) the issuance to the controlling interests of large numbers of stock-purchase warrants.

We also should not be surprised when financial heroes of the moment eventually turn out to be villains who contribute to the corruption of finance. In the eighteenth century, John Law rose to fame; he helped to stabilize the tottering financial situation in France by having his private bank redeem all of its notes in gold at a fixed rate. Yet he later fell into disrepute when he decided to devalue the currency, following a spectacular career in which he manipulated, among other things, the stock of his Mississippi Company. Charles Ponzi is noted for his financing scheme, wherein he paid off existing investors with new funds obtained from others until this pyramid finally fell apart in 1920. Ivan Kreuger, known as the Match King, was a powerful industrial leader in the early twentieth century, especially in the 1920s. He amassed huge debts to finance his sprawling empire in matches. However, much of the vital information regarding his companies and their assets was not documented, but rather was stored only in his head. Many confidants, subordinates, banks, and even some accountants never questioned his methods. When he committed suicide in 1932, he probably left behind the largest bankruptcy recorded up to that date.

The world of the late 1980s was, in many ways, strikingly different from the past. Rapid changes swept the landscape, and national governments found it increasingly difficult to cope in that environment. In this sense, the private sector was leading and governments were lagging. The integration of world economies continued at a fast clip. World markets established prices of commodities such as wheat, coal, and oil, along with clothing, automobiles, and semiconductors. Since the 1960s, satellites, fiber-optic communications, airplanes, and container ships had contributed much to a more integrated world economy. To my audience in 1988, the changes that had occurred in 20 years were hardly noticeable, but they were worth mentioning—for the historical perspective and reference.

On the financial side, one feature that distinguished this time from earlier periods was the rapid and large growth of debt, without intervening periods of debt rollbacks. This rapid increase had occurred in all major sectors—households, businesses, and government. During the 1980s alone, the growth of debt exceeded that of nominal gross national product (GNP)—an unprecedented trend. In earlier times, large increases in debt were stemmed by financial crises and panics, which induced large debt liquidations through bankruptcies and reorganizations. Although the United States had experienced several financial crises within the prior 25 years, the overall accumulation of debt continued unabated. The crises in those times were contained by improved official policy management and official international monetary cooperation to a larger degree than were crises in the pre–World War II period. The success of those policies, however, made market participants more confident. Few entities actually failed, and many survived.

The ability to overcome these crises thus contributed to the growth of debt and the liberalization of credit standards. We had come to accept the rapid growth of U.S. government debt, far beyond any level thought possible by policy makers just a decade or two earlier, and households and businesses had assumed debt burdens that absorbed huge shares of their income. Among our financial institutions, we had some very large banks that had bonds that barely merited investment-grade ratings and a few with bonds that had fallen below that level. Without deposit insurance, these institutions would have been out of business. How could they attract deposits at very low costs and make loans to borrowers who had credit ratings higher than the banks themselves?

In the business sector, in particular, the so-called decapitalization of corporations, mainly through the substitution of debt for equity through mergers and leveraged buyouts, became a dominant feature of corporate finance. From 1984 to 1988, this activity resulted in an unprecedented number of corporate bonds having their credit ratings downgraded. Indeed, the financial crises that took place in the 1960s and in 1970, when interest rates (by the standards of the day) were relatively low, made a greater impression on market participants than did the crises that occurred during that decade. For example, when, for the first time in the postwar period, institutions experienced substantial disintermediation during the credit crunch of 1966, fears abounded. A kind of a paralysis came over the financial markets, even though the prime loan rate at its peak reached only 6 percent and high-grade corporate bonds moved to 6.3 percent. When the Penn Central Railroad failed in 1970, the market went into deep shock. At the time of both crises, the financial system was closer to being immobilized than when the prime loan rate reached 21½ percent early in the 1980s.

Thus, it should not be surprising that the volatility of securities prices and of currencies had become a deeply rooted feature of our new financial world, and that this, too, was markedly different from earlier times—especially in the fixed-income markets. The dramatic increase in volatility is readily apparent if we consider the differences between the high and low yields of high-grade corporate bonds for each year since 1920. This difference averaged well under 50 basis points from 1920 through 1969, rose to 98 basis points in the 1970s, and then jumped to 273 basis points in the 1980s.

There were at least five causes for the dangerous volatility in securities and currency prices I pointed to at the time: I ranked as first and second of these causes financial deregulation and innovation. They combined to make money and credit highly mobile. Many securities were deemed marketable and readily priced; portfolio performance was monitored closely; and many derivative instruments—the simplest of which are futures and options—were created and could garner large rates of return (and also losses) through only moderate price movements. As the Brady Report of 1987 pointed out, some of the then new techniques, such as portfolio insurance, could exaggerate a near-term price trend even though the approach was supposed to limit the risk of the user.

Third, I also identified the globalization of financial markets as a major factor in increased volatility. The U.S. stock market did not collapse in a vacuum on October 19, 1987. On the contrary, major markets abroad all fell, and some plunged even more than the U.S. market. The withdrawal of investors from markets foreign to their own countries had a significant negative impact around the world. Similarly, foreign bond buyers exerted a powerful influence on the U.S. bond market. For example, when Japanese institutions were large buyers in the U.S. Treasury's quarterly financing operations, the bond market strengthened. When they and other foreign investors hesitated—as they do when the financing occurs during a period of U.S. dollar pressure in foreign exchange markets—the bond market quickly gave ground. Even foreign official institutions' buying of dollars to stabilize the price did not necessarily steady the price swings in securities markets for two reasons: Official intervention does not cure the fundamental underlying disequilibrium; and market participants may sell securities in anticipation of tighter monetary policy in the United States to ameliorate the imbalance.

Fourth, there was the secular underlying trend of the institutionalization of savings, which, combined with the increased securitization of markets, continued to contribute to big swings in market prices. Securitization is the vehicle through which financial assets can move in and out of institutional portfolios, and the institutionalization of savings is concentrating portfolio and investment decisions in the hands of fewer participants. Thus, we came to have a fundamental anomaly: On the one hand, the market, through securitization, created an increasing proportion of supposedly marketable credit instruments; on the other hand, the investment decision came to rest with large institutions rather than with a wide range of participants who may have held diverse market views. The Brady commission report hinted at this phenomenon when it described the hectic trading activities of that October shock. As this concentration of investment decision making continues through the institutionalization of savings, marketability, in its truest sense, will regress, and volatility will continue to rise until institutions and markets take on new forms and structures.

Finally, in the new financial world of the latter part of the twentieth century, the prices of securities had become much more a vehicle for trying to achieve economic stability. At first blush, this seems incongruous: the quest for economic stability through financial market volatility. But, as I pointed out in 1988, the reality is that there were no real financial circuit breakers that would assist the Federal Reserve in its task of stabilizing economic activity. Obviously, fiscal policy is not timely enough. Therefore, market participants had become extremely sensitive to the slightest shifts in monetary policy, both in the United States and abroad, as they tried to benefit by anticipating whether the Federal Reserve was moving toward higher or lower interest rates. As a result, I explained, we would continue to experience dramatic responses in market prices when the Fed eased or tightened.

The intransigence of volatility had also been a powerful contributor to the high level of inflation-adjusted (real) interest rates in that 1980s environment. Although there had never been a constant real interest rate, the high level of real rates at the time was nevertheless striking and markedly different from earlier periods.

Inflation-adjusted high-grade corporate bond yields had averaged 5.8 percent in the 1980s (a period in which volatility had been very high) and 1.1 percent in the 1960s and 1970s (a period in which yield volatility was moderate). It is, of course, reasonable to conclude that there will be additional compensation for the additional risk that results from increased volatility.

Where did this leave us in 1988 in terms of what to expect for the future? I then lectured and wrote that the transformation of the economic and financial markets would continue, and while the powerful forward movement of world economic and financial integration might occasionally face obstacles, the trend could not be denied.

The world would be linked even closer in the coming decades, as we reaped the benefits of ongoing technological progress. It seems almost quaint to recall that at the time some experts claimed that by the year 2000 microcomputers would be as powerful as a 1988 mainframe and that industrial countries would be covered by digital communication networks that communicate among businesses and homes with high-powered fiber-optic links.

Other economic developments would challenge our world. Despite improvements, manufacturing would not likely be a major factor in GNP growth over the 1990s. The shift of production from goods to services would continue. Economic development tends to follow an irregular trend from agriculture to manufacturing and then to services. I noted that we would have to adjust to significant changes in the labor force. According to studies being issued in the late 1980s, for the rest of that century the composition of the workforce would change more slowly than at any time since the 1930s. As a result, the average age of the working population would rise, and the number of young workers would shrink. Moreover, minorities would probably comprise a larger percentage of the newcomers into the labor force.

In the financial arena, harnessing the dynamism of the financial markets to the constructive use of society was an urgent problem that had to be addressed to avoid a major economic and financial calamity. The primary benefits of these changes are supposed to be lower financing costs and the offering of a wide range of investment alternatives to savers. Although these are laudable benefits, I told my audience that we could not afford to be beguiled by them.

In the new financial world, the fundamental issue is what mechanism to put in place to govern it effectively. Very little progress had been made on this front, because the real governor of a deregulated and competitive financial world is market discipline. Those who choose well will prosper and those who err will fail. In the financial markets, this discipline is not totally operative. The risk to society is deemed to be too high. The failures of large institutions, with numerous transactions and relationships with other institutions both in the United States and abroad, are considered essential and could induce systemic risks if allowed to flounder into bankruptcy. The arrangement at that time, therefore, encouraged excessive risk taking, because market discipline was not allowed to work and no other governing approach, through new forms of regulation, was being implemented quickly enough.

This problem was complicated by a group of archaic official regulatory and supervisory agencies. Most had segmented financial market responsibilities at a time when market segmentation was rapidly disappearing. Time would encourage an amalgamation of these supervisory responsibilities into one governing body over financial markets and institutions that can then promulgate integrated roles and conducts of financial behavior. And, I then hoped, such a change would occur before a major financial mishap.

Internationally, a similar, but more intricate, problem confronted us in 1988. Regardless of where domiciled, all major institutions and markets exhibited the complex interplay of money and credit. Nevertheless, there were vast differences among countries in terms of their trading practices, accounting and reporting standards, and capital requirements, among other things. Official international cooperation among major industrial nations would be helpful in dealing with these matters, but it would not be enough.

The dilemma in 1988 was this: How do we overcome the structural rigidities among nations to get the best out of the ongoing economic and financial changes? This is not to say that comparable problems did not exist in the past. The transition from feudalism to the nation-state that came into power with the industrial revolution was difficult, to be sure. However, changes in business and finance happened more quickly in the late twentieth century (and now) and therefore required more finely honed and timely reforms in national policies. Instead, we heard new voices with old themes and prescriptions, especially on economic matters. Fair trade instead of free trade is not a new concept. Calls for denying foreign dollar holders the freedom to express their investment choices are just another step backwards. In the financial arena, it would probably take a long time before the key industrial countries would be willing to relinquish some sovereignty to an official international institution that could oversee and set uniform rules and regulations for all key markets and institutions.

In the meantime, financial markets would continue to be highly volatile. All the forces that contribute to volatility remained operative: financial deregulation, innovation, the trend toward financial globalization, the institutionalization of savings, and a monetary approach that requires huge swings in the value of financial assets to stabilize economic behavior. Prices of financial assets were bound to flare with shifts in monetary policy, around cyclical turning points in the economy and in response to market bubbles, which were likely to be an endemic feature of our new financial world.

The setting in 1988 raised perplexing issues for the Federal Reserve. Could the Fed, for example, correctly gauge the market's response to a tightening of policy and the consequences for the economy of such tightening actions? When the Fed firmed policy in 1987 in response to the weakening dollar and heightening inflation expectations, the negative market reaction was concentrated in the fixed-income markets for nearly a half a year, while the stock market crumbled only belatedly. The quick, substantial monetary easing that followed in late October 1987, together with other factors, muted the impact on the economy. A business recession was averted, and inflation expectations were dampened.

However, the likely firming in monetary policy in 1988 would take place under somewhat different circumstances. Considering the political realities of 1988 and the uncertainties about the economy, a firming in policy would come reluctantly—and only when resource utilization rose and renewed inflation actually showed up in the numbers.

Nevertheless, any delay in monetary firming, or the prospect of a delay, would not be ignored by the bond market. Given the different environment in 1988, the stock market would not be likely to stand by idly as long as it did in 1987 before it reacted adversely again. A synchronized drop of bond and stock prices could thus provide the early warning sign of another business recession.

For the Federal Reserve, the new financial landscape would also mean that its function as lender of last resort would expand, unless we accepted the discipline of the marketplace, which was highly unlikely. This would reflect the blurring of distinctions among institutions, the continued large volume of open market transactions, and efforts to hold marketable assets rather than longer-term financial arrangements. These, during moments of difficulty, would force the Fed to intervene and provide comfort beyond the traditional commercial banking link. Moreover, as long as the U.S. dollar continued as the key reserve currency, the Federal Reserve would also have to be a much bigger international lender of last resort, which could become extremely difficult as long as the rapid changes in the international financial markets outpaced the skills, the knowledge base, and the authority of the prevailing informal cooperative effort among central banks.

Events eventually tend to meet countervailing forces, and the financial world is no exception. One of these was a massive consolidation of financial institutions as a result of increased deregulation, innovation, and technological costs of doing business. Having let the genie out of the bottle, many traditional financial institutions had assets and liabilities that served them well in the segmented markets of prior times but that were cost-embedded and came to create new losses. They would not survive the changes that were under way.

To the Federal Reserve, an eventually greater concentration of financial institutions would ease the complexity of monetary policy for two reasons. First, by definition, it is easier to carry out policy effectively when it involves few instead of many. Second, the huge financial institutions that I saw coming would be vertically integrated, thereby keeping in-house many activities that in the mid-1980s were transacted in the open credit markets. Thus, financial concentration would ultimately diminish open market activity. Although a financial system dominated by a few large institutions could make it easier for the Fed to implement policy, it might not serve the public best. The financial system would be less competitive and one step removed from substantial government domination.

In 1988 I suggested that the first evidence of greater government involvement in the marketplace was probably only a few years away, and that it would occur when the next recession hit. Alleviating the debt burden would be difficult in the short run. Never in the postwar period had so many been so excessively leveraged. The entire explosion of the high-yield, low-quality junk bond market was the product of the economic expansion of that time. And while financial institutions still held a large and questionable volume of foreign loans, they were massive lenders to a deteriorating corporate sector. At a minimum, monetary policy would have to ease decisively and broaden the official safety net. Moreover, monetary policy would probably have the sole burden of resuscitating the economy. Fiscal policy may not be sufficiently stimulative right away, because the U.S. government would have a huge budget deficit of its own before the start of the next recession.

The transformation of financial markets is a natural attribute of a changing world. After all, the essence of life is continuous change. Nevertheless, we should be aware of whether what we consider to be new has actually occurred before. At a minimum, poor financial practices should not be repeated. Here, knowledge of history can be instructive. The profound financial changes that came about in the 1980s posed substantial challenges that needed to be addressed: (1) the rapid growth of debt, which was generally deteriorating in quality; (2) the sharp increase in the volatility of financial assets and currencies; (3) the absence of effective official governing bodies for markets and institutions both in the United States and abroad; and (4) the lack of a code of conduct in the financial markets.

A code of conduct is as essential for financial markets as it is for society as a whole. After all, we in financial markets have a great public trust. We hold the savings and temporary funds for all of society. How well we carry out this responsibility has a great impact on economic progress and, as history clearly shows, we in the financial markets will never escape public scrutiny and judgment.

# 2

# *Reflections on Business, the Lessons of History, and Globalization*

Business and financial markets affect the lives of every American in very real ways. Each of us needs to make some sense of the whirlwind of economic and financial information swirling around us. We are deluged by torrents of economic and financial information, by analyses, forecasts, and interpretations—most of it real-time—a flood far broader and deeper than anything I was confronted with when I began my career many decades ago. In the 1960s, instantaneous financial information was a privileged and limited resource for Wall Street elites; today, millions tune in to TV and radio stations devoted entirely to up-to-the-second financial news. In the immediate postwar years, few outside economics and finance could have named the chairman of the Federal Reserve; today, the Fed chairman is an international celebrity, considered by many to be second only to the president of the United States in power and influence.

This dramatic thickening and acceleration of financial and economic information is, of course, an outgrowth of vast improvements in communications, of the geometric expansion of computing power, and of the rapid spread of powerful new quantitative analytical techniques among securities traders and investors. The volume of marketable securities that are revalued with lightning rapidity has grown beyond almost anyone's imagination. And the changes have been qualitative as well as quantitative; the very structure and, to some extent, the behavior of markets have changed as well.

How are we to understand these changes? Does historical experience hold the key? I am a great believer in the value of history—in finance and business, as in all aspects of life. But I want to reflect for a few moments on the limits of historical analogy.

To begin, it is important to recognize that change is the essence of life, in professional life as well as personal life. We cannot freeze time. We cannot undo the past. Nor do we relive the past in any precise manner. While it can be useful to search for patterns that can inform current circumstances and that might even provide some guideposts for the future, it is essential to recognize that the differences between past and present far outweigh the similarities. Following the Great Crash of 1929, the best financial minds erroneously deemed it "another 1921," referring to the deep but short-lived recession that had followed World War I. Similarly, many experts declared the 1987 stock market crash "another 1929." The first misappropriation of history led to overly optimistic expectations; the latter, to unnecessarily dire predictions.

Historical reflection also seems chronically prone to nostalgia. By most measures, however, the so-called good old days were not so good. Globally and in the United States, average standards of living are much higher today than they were only a few decades ago. Americans are living much longer—and remaining healthy and active longer—than our parents and grandparents. The world has become more tolerant and more democratic. It is much harder for totalitarian regimes to maintain monopoly control over information and insulate their societies. Poverty, injustice, and violence remain all too common, but few would trade places with their ancestors if given the chance.

History should teach us that projecting the future by merely extending the past is a risky exercise. To be sure, over a long stretch of time the U.S. economy has grown enormously. So has the world economy, though not as robustly. But when we telescope in for a closer look, we see amazing variation in economic performance and financial behavior from one decade to the next.

Consider the eventful and never-predictable twentieth century. It began in an atmosphere of industrial triumph and international cooperation, but that was soon shattered by the First World War. Then came unprecedented speculation in the 1920s, worldwide depression in the 1930s, another global conflagration in the 1940s, economic recovery and rehabilitation in the 1950s, growth and the unleashing of inflation in the 1960s, and global energy shocks and stagflation in the 1970s. In the 1980s, disinflation and financial deregulation swept across the American economy, while Japan and Germany were seen as the economic models of the future. The 1990s brought the fall of the Soviet Union; the return of American political, economic, and financial dominance; and a new wave of materialism, speculation, and other excesses in the financial markets. Ten decades—each as different from the previous one as anyone could imagine, although precious few could or did imagine what the next decade would bring as the twentieth century lurched forward.

When we look to the future, there is a natural tendency to over-extrapolate from the immediate, lived past. This encourages simplistic judgments. When conditions are good, the inclination is to conclude they will get even better, and in bad times the fear is they will get worse. Such fashions in economic judgments can be harmful. They can raise false expectations about unsustainable business momentum, either up or down.

The same can be said about trajectories in life: Trends are made to be broken. One should not assume steady progress toward one's goals. I learned firsthand that career paths could take many detours. My family's ambition was for me to become a doctor of medicine. But as I struggled through an intensive summer course in chemistry during my freshman year in college, it became abundantly clear to me that I would never take the Hippocratic oath. Instead, I found a different path and became a doctor, not of medicine, but of banking and finance—and probably the first PhD economist to work on Wall Street.

As I mentioned earlier, financial institutions play an enveloping role in modern life, and it is one of our challenges to navigate our way through the thicket. Financial institutions hold the savings and temporary funds of households, business corporations, and governments. They intermediate the flow of money and credit. Typically, they have huge liabilities and assets, but a relatively small capital base. By their very nature, they use other people's money. If financial institutions are to perform well, they must balance their fiduciary responsibility with their entrepreneurial drive. It is an exquisitely difficult balancing act.

Too often, the basic fiduciary duty of financial institutions has been eclipsed in the high-voltage, high-velocity environment that has emerged in recent decades. With financial assets extraordinarily mobile, with growing access to debt by borrowers, and with the absorbing excitement of the trading floor—which for some becomes a sort of game, an end in itself—the notion of financial trusteeship frequently gets lost in the melee.

The shabby events of the recent past demonstrate that people in finance cannot and should not escape public scrutiny. The magnitude of the recent financial laxity is appalling. In the first five years of this decade alone, financial institutions paid more than $22 billion in fines for an assortment of transgressions. Who should be held accountable? Most immediately, senior managers of financial institutions must bear part of the responsibility. Too many have sanctioned imprudent and unlawful practices, lured by huge near-term profits and by the generous benefits that come with them. Accounting standards have been compromised, sometimes seriously, as managers, financial officers, and their advisers have inflated balance sheets by pricing assets and liabilities incorrectly. Conflicts of interest in financing and investment relationships have become almost commonplace.

Business schools have played a role in the breakdown of responsible financial behavior in how they structure their curricula. According
to a recent study of business and financial history taught in business
schools, there has been a downward trend over the past two decades.
Today, our system of higher education rarely teaches financial history,
or even business and economic history for that matter. Earlier in the
preceding century, business majors at most colleges and universities were
required to take courses in business and financial history, while the history of economics and economic thought was a staple in economics
programs. This is no longer the case. In their entrancement with new
quantitative methods, most business schools long ago abandoned their
historically oriented courses, not merely as requirements, but as elec-
tives as well. Anything having to do with the qualitative side of business
practice—ethics, business culture, history, and the like—was subordi-
nated or eliminated as being too "soft" and "impractical." In doing so,
business schools have catered to the immediate needs and demands of
the financial markets and have forsaken some of their broader responsibilities. Yet we are surprised when the senior managers of financial
institutions that go astray hold good academic credentials.

Ironically, the recent wave of corporate scandals seems to have
inspired some business schools to reintroduce some elective courses in
ethics and business history. This is not enough, though. Business schools
should require all degree candidates to take courses in business and
financial history.

Financial excesses should be constrained not only by market
actors, but also by government regulators, especially within the Federal
Reserve System. This is because excessive credit creation breeds excessive credit practices in the private sector. The fundamental objective of
monetary policy is to balance sustainable economic growth with price
stability. But most central bankers associate price stability with the stability of goods and services.

Excessive inflation in financial asset prices, while appealing to short-
term investors, can be corrosive over time. It can breed excesses in

business investment. It can contribute to undue economic and financial concentration. It can encourage questionable flows of funds into risky markets at the hands of inexperienced investors. In short, excessive inflation in financial asset prices can undermine the foundation of a stable economy.

The record shows that when asset values have fallen suddenly, the Fed has eased monetary policy to provide greater liquidity to the financial markets and to counteract the decline in domestic spending that might result from the loss of financial wealth. But when asset prices have advanced strongly, driving up financial wealth and encouraging looser investment practices, the Federal Reserve generally has not responded in a timely fashion by tightening monetary policy. This asymmetry, in turn, has encouraged the expectation that the central bank will bail out large, overextended institutions. The Fed ultimately might correct this policy blind spot, but experience suggests it may not act before another round of financial adversity forces the issue.

An important dimension of the economic and financial complexities that surround us is, of course, globalization. The term has become popular recently, but globalization itself has been ongoing for centuries. Business and financial global interdependence has accelerated recently because of improved communication and transportation, as well as the application of new technology in manufacturing and service sectors. In the long run, the nations that benefit most from globalization will be those that come closest to attaining the ideal of economic democracy. In those countries, impartiality rather than social democracy is the dominant guiding principle; equality of opportunity, not equality of outcome, takes precedence. Social democrats look to legislatures, elected officials, and elite bureaucrats to determine economic and financial outcomes. In economic democracies, market forces determine such outcomes.

Competing effectively in today's globalization requires labor mobility, educational competence, efficient capital markets, and, above all, the willingness among all sectors of society to accept and adjust to changing conditions. It is unrealistic to believe that societies will adjust smoothly to the rigors of globalization. Socialistic societies will be hindered by their efforts to protect economic sectors that cannot compete effectively in global markets. Authoritarian governments will fail because they are inefficient allocators of economic resources.

How will the United States fare? After all, the glory of Greece and Rome did not endure; and in more recent times, the power and reach of Spain, Holland, and even Great Britain did not stand the test of time. Some now postulate that the United States will lose its superpower status as this century matures. They call attention to two challenges. First is the considerable challenge we face in coming to grips with our twin deficit problem—our federal budget deficit and the deficit in our balance of payments. The second challenge is related to some extent to the first: Will the United States continue to thrive in the face of globalization, especially if China emerges, as many predict it will, as the next superpower?

I doubt that the U.S. dollar will be dethroned as the world's key reserve currency anytime soon. While some realignment in currency values is likely, the American economy is underpinned by a stable and strong political system, by financial institutions that are larger and stronger than those in other parts of the industrial world, and by profitable and highly competitive investment returns when adjusted for global risks. The economic and financial gaps between the United States and China will remain wide for some time to come. The average gross domestic product (GDP) per person in China is $5,000, compared with $38,000 in the United States. China's banking system is highly fragmented, opaque, and financially strained and weak. The United States has 4,000 accredited higher schools of learning; China has only about 350. Nearly 600,000 foreign students study in the United States, compared with only 78,000 in China.

The United States does not possess a pure form of market capitalism, nor does it claim to. Even so, our economic democracy is closer to that ideal than virtually any other major political economy in the world today. That difference—embodied in the spirit of equal opportunity, in the opportunity to persist and to succeed, in the ability to move through the social structure, and in the pluralism of our society—will enable us to remain the global leader.

For me, the defining attributes of this country that I just spoke about—opportunity, pluralism, and social mobility—were not abstract concepts. They were everyday realities, but they allowed me to pursue my aspirations. Today, these attributes of American life are even more vivid and distinctive than they were when I came here as a boy.

# 3

# *If Adam Smith Were Alive Today*

Adam Smith of Scotland is arguably the greatest economist who ever lived. His classic *The Wealth of Nations* appeared the year of the American Revolutionary War, and is unsurpassed in the history of economic thought for its erudition. Modern economists display nothing close to Smith's range in the subjects they engage. I was especially honored, therefore, when in 2001 I was presented with the Adam Smith Award by the National Association for Business Economics in New York City. The occasion inspired me to engage in a thought experiment. What could we learn about how our economy has changed since 1776, about its key strengths and weaknesses, by imagining what Smith would perceive if he were to survey contemporary Wall Street and the larger financial scene? I suspect that Smith would find much to applaud about our capitalist system, but also much to lament, especially in the massive consolidation of our financial institutions.

A remarkable individual, Smith left an indelible imprint on economic thought. He differed in many ways from the modern-day economist. As measured by our contemporary standards, Adam Smith received no formal training, much less a PhD in economics, which was not available at the time. Instead, he studied mathematics, the natural sciences, philosophy, and classical writings. In Smith's day, the well-educated were not confined within rigid disciplinary boundaries like they are today. The world is better for it, for we can see the erudition of Smith's reading reflected clearly in the comprehensiveness of his economic thought.

At the age of 27, Smith became professor of moral philosophy at Glasgow University, where he delved into questions of moral philosophy and political economy. At Glasgow, Smith emerged as a very popular teacher. As one historian noted, "a multitude of students from a great distance resorted to the University merely upon his account." Today, many academicians place their research interests far above their engagement with students. Of course, research is vital for the advancement of economic knowledge. Still, today's scholars need to give greater emphasis to their classroom exchange with students. After all, who doesn't recall from his or her college days the outstanding lectures, the extraordinary capacity of a professor to simplify complex matters, and the special mentor who generously gave us individual attention?

Adam Smith would readily understand the fact that academic life today is driven by a "publish or perish" mentality, which essentially is a market-driven phenomenon. The scholar builds a national reputation through publication, whereas even the most outstanding teaching can affect only a local student audience.

But consider the fact that Adam Smith actually published only two works in his lifetime. The first was *The Theory of Moral Sentiment*, which he published at the age of 36. Although that work is hardly remembered today, it was an investigation of considerable range and insight that earned Smith great renown in his day. In *The Theory of Moral Sentiment*, he expounded on such matters as the propriety of action, the objects of reward and punishment, the character of virtue, and the practice of philosophy. These are hardly the subjects economists would delve into today. Nevertheless, Smith's early explorations in moral sentiment served as a foundation for his magnum opus, *The Wealth of Nations*, which the 53-year-old Scottish social philosopher published in 1776. Written in a grand style—and completely free of the kind of mathematical apparatus common to today's learned journals—*The Wealth of Nations* has endured the test of time. Born the same year as the world's greatest capitalist nation, it remains one of the most perceptive and influential works of the modern age.

Central to Smith's treatise was his eloquent argument that it is part of human nature to strive for economic growth and that this can best be achieved through unfettered competition, the division of labor, and free trade. As we all know, Adam Smith believed that the state should play a very limited role. For him, governments should be properly confined to safeguarding society from violence and invasions, to protecting every member of society from injustice and oppression, and to providing certain public works and institutions. At the same time, he warned that "No society can surely be flourishing and happy of which the far greater part of the members are poor and miserable." It is interesting to note that Smith did not favor a flat tax. He was very specific in this matter: "The subjects of every state," he wrote, "ought to contribute towards the support of government, as nearly as possible in proportion to their respective abilities."

What would Adam Smith say about economic and financial developments since his death in 1796? He would no doubt applaud the rise in living standards and the rapid industrialization in many parts of the world that have been driven by the kinds of innovations and division of labor that Smith advocated, yet far beyond even his imaginings. Even just a century ago, the average U.S. industrial worker toiled 10 hours a day, six days a week, to bring home a mere $375 a year. At that time, working conditions were typically unsanitary, unsafe, and often fatal, and there were few protections. Among American males of all occupations 100 years ago, whites lived an average of only 47 years, blacks a mere 33. In Adam Smith's day it took Thomas Jefferson and John Adams six full weeks to cross the Atlantic; today we can make the trip in seven hours.

Adam Smith wrote a lot about the importance of information in ensuring the smooth and efficient operation of markets. But he could hardly anticipate the advent of instantaneous communications, beginning with the telegraph and telephone in the nineteenth century, much less today's Internet and World Wide Web. And how could even a visionary mind like Adam Smith's have imagined the coming of bio-technology—from high-tech pharmaceuticals to genetic engineering—or electronics and miniaturization?

Adam Smith would have applauded the expansion of free trade among nations during the past two centuries. He believed that the bigger the market, the greater the division of labor within countries, and thus the greater the economic benefit for all involved. He believed that tariffs and subsidies divert capital investment away from the most productive sectors of the economy and toward the most inefficient ones.

So how far have we truly come along Adam Smith's economic path? At first blush, the defeat of communism (as symbolized by the collapse of the Soviet Union) was a victory for capitalism. Karl Marx was proven wrong. A system in which most property and the means of production were owned by the state, in which most economic activities were centrally planned by government officials, and in which goods and services were produced by the citizens of the state and distributed among the citizens by the government simply failed to work.

While Adam Smith would have greeted the defeat of communism with great delight as a vindication of his economic philosophy, he would nevertheless quickly note—as he did in his writings—that the potential *excesses* of capitalism could be very dangerous. Remember, Smith believed in a system that encourages individuals to pursue their self-interest and that society will benefit as long as self-interest is restrained by competition. He warned that competition could be compromised by collusion, monopolistic practices, and limitations on international trade.

Today, the United States comes closest to the kind of economic society envisioned by Adam Smith. Yet we are still far from what he prescribed. We aspire to live in what I call an economic democracy, in which equal opportunity and not equality of outcome takes precedence. The idealistic American view looks to market forces to determine economic outcomes and accepts the fact that great economic disparities between winners and losers are a normal consequence of the free market system. In contrast, in the social democracies around the world, legislatures, elected officials, and elite bureaucrats play important roles in the economic decision-making process. In Europe, the political emphasis is on social justice and fair trade, and on an economic system aimed at producing a kinder and gentler outcome than is suggested, at first glance, by a highly competitive market-driven society.

In Japan, an economic system run through a consensus approach still holds great appeal. Even after a decade of virtually no economic growth, many Japanese still believe that their society and culture are based on a foundation of harmony. In Japan and in Europe, the tight interplay among big government, big business, and big labor all combine to limit the freedom of decision making, the mobility of labor, and the incentives of business to excel. These features induce a rigidity that Adam Smith would abhor.

Adam Smith also would have cheered the globalization of business activity, in which the United States has been a leader in the post–World War II years. This is because the underlying premise of globalization is that it maximizes comparative advantages and therefore produces goods and services at the lowest cost. For quite a while, the main thrust of globalization for Americans, Europeans, and Japanese was to establish or acquire foreign facilities in order to be closer to sources of labor, raw materials, or customers. In the past few decades, another development has enhanced globalization—namely, the increase in the mobility of labor. Political freedom has spread into Eastern Europe and Russia. China has become more politically open-minded. Transportation and communication have improved vastly. All of these developments are encouraging individuals to seek an improved return for their labor. While the United States always has been more favorably inclined toward immigration, Europe and Japan have not. To be sure, the United States limits immigration, but the integration of immigrants into the mainstream of our society is one of its distinguishing features. That cannot be said of Europe generally and of Japan particularly. Immigrants there are tolerated rather than embraced. It is difficult for them to acquire new citizenship. And their presence invites outbursts of nationalism and social unrest, especially during business slowdowns. I suspect that Adam Smith would say, "How can there be efficient globalized markets when capital is free to move and labor mobility is restrained?"

Thus, it would seem that if globalization of business and financial activity were pursued along the philosophical views of Adam Smith, much good ought to come of it. It would create a strong dynamic for change and efficiency. It would tend to promote a better allocation of resources at the company, global, and national levels. It would foster innovations and competitiveness. It would improve decision-making capabilities because investors would receive full information from companies and punish issuers of securities who try to subvert the company. It would broaden risk taking across society and breed a healthy awareness of profits.

But we are nowhere near that ideal economic system. Today, our economic system is infused with a wide range of checks and balances on the behavior of business and financial enterprises. Even after a generation of deregulation, our system is honeycombed with regulations through our tax codes, social safety nets for citizens, and industries that are deemed to have special needs. At the local, state, and federal levels, government plays an active role in economic affairs, sometimes helping to improve economic efficiency but very often interfering, with detrimental consequences.

Nor does our system tolerate well the harshest of competitive outcomes—business failure—especially when it comes to the largest corporations, banks, and other enterprises. In our imperfect economic democracy, these entities are, in effect, too big to fail. Historically, when they have gotten into serious trouble, the government—weighing the immediate social and economic costs—has tended to step in to shore up the faltering giants with loan guarantees, tax breaks, and other subsidies. Under the strict rules of market capitalism, such firms would be left on their own to endure the rigors of market discipline. Indeed, Adam Smith would argue that faltering firms are, by definition, weaker firms, and that their failures are good for the economy. The fact is global free trade is more of a slogan than a reality. Whenever there is a significant economic slowdown, the proponents of managed trade and fair trade come to the fore.

Although Smith would applaud some aspects of today's global financial markets, he would find others quite troubling. Surely, he would have lamented the massive expansion of securitized credit that, among other things, ushered in the financial crisis of 2007. *The Wealth of Nations* contains many cautionary notes about the risks of unregulated paper money and credit issuance. When banks issue paper money far in excess of their hard currency, he warned, they become vulnerable to runs. Smith also called for, in effect, the ongoing separation of commercial and investment banking. As Michael Mussa has noted in a perceptive essay about Smith's views in relation to modern finance, "Smith recommended . . . an 18th century version of the Glass-Steagall Act" and stressed that a "merry-go-round of money and credit becomes even more dangerous when it becomes opaque through the involvement of many different banks."

In that way, Smith was pointing toward another powerful trend today that, in the long run, will drastically reduce competition and turn us completely away from any tendencies toward economic democracy. This is the massive consolidation that is taking place in business and finance. Of course, Adam Smith's opposition to monopolies and their practices was unequivocal. In the past few decades, mergers have taken on huge proportions and have encompassed nonfinancial sectors such as airlines, autos, chemicals, communications, oil, natural gas, and health care. And they have reached beyond national borders into the global sphere.

We often hear the argument that these consolidations are driven by very large capital requirements. That may be valid for some businesses, especially in view of the rapidity of technological changes. But two other driving forces are more likely. First, consolidation gives managers an opportunity to reduce costs, increase profits, and in some cases improve customer service—all laudable goals. But huge consolidations also give the surviving firms greater control over the prices charged to customers and over the entire innovative process. All of this has the effect of reducing competition and impairing economic democracy.

I am especially concerned about the many adverse consequences that will come over the next few decades as rapid consolidation continues in the financial sector. Here are just a few examples of what has already happened. In the early 1980s, the top 10 U.S. banks held 19 percent of insured deposits of commercial banks. This percentage rose to more than 40 percent in 2000. In the mutual funds industry, the 25 largest mutual fund organizations held more than 70 percent of all mutual fund assets during the same period. These contraction ratios are likely to rise rapidly in this decade. Huge financial conglomerates have emerged that encompass banking, insurance, leasing, investment banking, securities trading, financial asset management, consumer financing, and credit card entities.

What are the challenges posed by these huge institutions? To begin with, they are extremely difficult to manage. In the long run, this will decrease economic efficiency. The wide range of financial activities prevents senior management from playing much of a direct role in day-to-day operations. As a result, senior managers become increasingly dependent on middle managers, many of whom are highly skilled at econometric techniques and motivated to take increasing risks to achieve higher compensation for themselves. These kinds of techniques—such as value-at-risk formulations—are heavily influenced by historical inputs, and thus can never fully assess the totality of risk taking. But senior managers find them reassuring.

The dangers of this kind of limited analysis are demonstrated vividly by recent financial crises. Simply put, the rapid pace and complexity of change in today's financial markets makes many rules of thumb and historical benchmarks obsolete. Replacing common sense with vigorous quantification is not the answer.

Second, financial conglomeration is riddled by conflicts of interest, conflicts that reduce the choices of borrowers and investors.

For example, while financial behemoths may offer one-stop financing, they often do so not as a choice but as part of the deal. Such institutions provide the borrower with a variety of loan facilities, underwritings, and asset management. As financial concentration continues, the customer not only will have fewer opportunities to shop for financing packages but will find few places in the market that will provide financing costs for each service.

This conflict of interest has now come to the fore in the research activities of financial conglomerates. It has become quite obvious that the research effort has often been compromised because of the pressure to support trading and underwriting activities. The problem will worsen as financial conglomeration intensifies.

The third challenge posed by financial and business conglomerates is that they are deemed too big to fail. There have been quite a few instances of governmentally assisted bailouts because the institution involved posed a systemic risk or the debtors involved were vital to our national interest. No matter how one examines this approach, the too-big-to-fail approach skews the economic system in favor of bigness and weakens the market's competitive process.

Increased financial concentration will have a profound effect on market activity itself. Eventually, the breadth and depth of the secondary markets will diminish. With fewer participants, whom do you really trade with? How can you make effective markets when there are relatively few buyers or sellers? As a result, the accuracy of marking portfolios to market will become questionable. The contagion effect, as it is talked about today, will move to a much higher level as huge institutions straddle the globe with generally uniform rather than diverse mind-sets.

Unfortunately, there is little popular political or governmental opposition to consolidation to compare with the contentious antitrust movement of a century ago. Today, mergers often are justified as a way of meeting international competition. Politicians tend to have little motivation to take on the big interests, especially when there is little public support to do so. The public's attitude has shifted dramatically from a century ago, when large businesses were owned or controlled privately. Today, many households invest in stocks and reap immediate benefits from mergers. Moreover, the problem I am describing does not get full attention, because our current drift away from economic democracy is gradual rather than abrupt. The prevailing attitude is: "Let someone else tackle the problem."

It is also unfortunate that central bankers do not meet the too-big-to-fail problem head-on. They do not want to recognize the subtle ways in which financial competition is diminishing. Conflicts of interest do not receive high priority in their decisions. Periods of monetary restraint frequently result in the disappearance of smaller and medium-sized financial institutions, leaving only a handful of very large ones. Central bankers are not sufficiently concerned about the moral hazard underlying the too-big-to-fail approach. They claim that when a large financial institution gets into trouble, the stockholders and lenders are forced to accept losses and the senior management may also be removed.

This is hardly a forward-thinking approach. Too-big-to-fail institutions can contribute to massive excessive debt creation and to a serious weakening of the credit structure before the central bank intervenes to stop them from failing.

The very complexity in the structure of large financial institutions, combined with the complacency born of the too-big-to-fail philosophy, invites aggressive risk taking. Incentives to leverage always will overshadow prudent judgments. In these circumstances, the power of central banking actually increases rather than diminishes, and central bankers are lauded as heroes who headed off economic calamity. But the competence of our central banks should be judged by how well they have managed to contain financial excesses.

Adam Smith's writing on this issue more than two centuries ago—when financial markets were embryonic compared with today—was quite visionary. He said, "The state should give monopolies to no one, but should encourage the creation of as many as possible. In this way, the bad consequences of the errors of speculation of a few banks, resulting in their ruin, would be dispersed throughout the system so that no serious damage could result."

Whereas Adam Smith perceived and warned against the key threats to the market system in his day, today there is no comparable clarion call warning us of the threats to our imperfect democracy and our economic and political way of life. As we continue to drift toward global business and financial consolidation over the next few decades, a new and powerful alignment will take place between big business, big government, and a newly shaped labor force. Economic and financial freedom will be constrained. Large private institutions will look more like public utilities than the independent organizations they aspire to be at present. What is needed now to begin to arrest this drift is a modern-day Adam Smith who will put forward an integrated view of this new economic and financial world of ours.

# PART II
# NEGLECTED
# EARLY WARNINGS

# 4

# Troubling Trends in Financial Markets and Official Policies

*In this overview for a symposium on "Restructuring the Financial System" in 1987, I issued a number of warnings about emerging trends—warnings that unfortunately proved to be prophetic, especially after the current financial crisis erupted. Among the key issues I raised were: Where does risk ultimately reside? What happens when commercial banks and other leading financial institutions become excessively entrepreneurial? Can deregulation go too far? The forum was the famed annual gathering of leading economists and policy makers (sponsored by the Federal Reserve Bank of Kansas City) in Jackson Hole, Wyoming.*

Extraordinary changes are taking place in the financial markets, and Congress and regulators are slow in responding to these changes. Simply put, our financial system is going astray. Many deposit institutions are weak, and businesses and households have assumed massive debt burdens. This poses serious risks for our economy. In light of these risks, the current system of financial regulation is inadequate to deal with changes in financial markets. Congress should abandon the current system and pass comprehensive legislation to install a better one.

In designing a better regulatory environment, we must ask ourselves what kind of a financial system we really want. What should the financial institutions and markets try to achieve? How can this be accomplished effectively while safeguarding the public trust? Are there important distinguishing aspects between financial institutions and other private enterprises in the economy? In other words, we should begin setting forth a rationale for our financial system and then establish some of the tenets that will move us closer to an improved financial regulatory structure.

To begin, let me say that it would be impossible to run our complex and advanced economy effectively without integrated supportive activity from financial institutions and markets whose role is to intermediate the savings and investment process. Financial institutions and markets reconcile the needs of both the demanders and the suppliers of funds. If we did not have an efficient financial system, the behavior of spending units and of savers would be severely limited and our economic performance would be sharply curtailed. Among other things, a well-functioning financial system should facilitate stable economic growth. In a broader sense, it should promote reasonable financial practices and curb excesses.

Some members of the financial and academic community make an important distinction regarding the underlying functions of the financial system. They divide the functions into two parts: to provide a mechanism through which flow all payments and to provide the framework through which allocating credit is efficient. This distinction is made because there is a clear need to safeguard the payments mechanism, but it is less clear that our system of credit allocation requires such safeguards. I believe, however, that in the financial world today, these functions are intertwined. The differences between money and credit are blurred. In an attitude that has changed markedly over the past few decades, borrowings are considered by many to be a source of liquidity and, therefore, a substitute for money or highly liquid assets. Short-term assets like Treasury bills and commercial paper are considered substitutes for money. Thus, the greater risks that may be inherent in today's credit structure are not reduced by paying special attention to safeguarding the payments mechanism, which once upon a time was a cash-only function. Moreover, other important financial changes have taken place that have affected the functioning of our financial system and that have often induced regulatory responses without full thought to the ultimate consequences. I will briefly mention five developments that need to be incorporated in plans to improve our financial system.

First, financial institutions today primarily acquire funds by bidding in the open market. This bidding for funds has been partly responsible for blurring the differences among financial institutions. A broad menu of obligations is available to temporary holders of funds and savers. Many are highly knowledgeable about these instruments and markets. Few institutions hold much in the way of captive funds at below-market yields.

Second, institutions and other participants in the financial markets now actively engage in spread banking—an effort through which institutions try to lock in a rate of return that exceeds the cost of their liabilities. This practice began years ago as a commercial banking technique, but other institutions and businesses have followed suit with the creation of many new credit instruments ranging from floating-rate obligations to interest-rate and currency swaps.

Third, these spread banking and related opportunities were greatly enhanced through securitization—which, as is well known, is the process by which a nonmarketable asset is turned into a marketable instrument. Today, many credit instruments have been securitized, including consumer credit obligations, mortgages, high-yield corporate bonds, and many derivative instruments, such as options and futures. They have enhanced the growth of the open market and inhibited the growth of the traditional banking market. Yet, many of these instruments, new as they are, are not completely understood and have yet to be tested in both bull and bear markets.

Fourth, financial institutions and markets are much more international in their activities. Funds flow from one country to another electronically with extraordinary volume, sometimes moving counter to underlying trade developments. Facilitating these international flows, large U.S. commercial banks and investment banks have built up great operations in key foreign money centers, and concurrently, foreign financial institutions are enjoying an increased presence in the United States. Today, many U.S. borrowers participate in both U.S. and foreign financial markets, and U.S. institutional investors are becoming more familiar with international opportunities. Again, the opportunity for reward has carried risk. Our money center banks' experience in lending to developing countries is one example. Managing the risk of floating exchange rates in a world of 24-hour-a-day trading is another.

Fifth, vast improvements in computer and communications technology are rendering many traditional institutional arrangements obsolete. Technological breakthroughs have a significant impact on the location of physical facilities, the communications linkages with clients, and the magnitude and speed of market decision making.

These changes, to a large extent, reflect the deregulation of interest rates without putting into place concurrently new prudential safeguards. In view of these developments, a number of issues need to be raised and resolved. One is whether financial institutions should be subject to special regulatory treatment. My answer is yes. This is because financial institutions are entrusted with an extraordinary public responsibility. They have a fiduciary role as the holders of the public's temporary funds and savings. They generally have large liabilities (other people's money) and a small capital base and are involved in allocating the proceeds from these liabilities to numerous activities that are critical to the functioning of our economy.

If the role of the financial system carries a public or fiduciary responsibility, as I believe it does, then a governmental role in guiding the system is valid. No highly developed society has treated financial institutions and markets as a strictly private activity, and Congress itself has long since recognized the role of central banking in guiding our financial system.

This distinction also hinges on the necessity for keeping the ownership of a financial enterprise separate from that of business and commercial activity. To combine the two would surely lead to economic and financial concentration, to major conflicts of interest, and to a compromise of the public responsibility of financial institutions. Equally important is that a marriage of business and the financial system would substantially widen the official financial safety net that is now extended only selectively to businesses and institutions when financial difficulties erupt. A mix of commerce and finance would spread the safety net to cover many private large enterprises. This, in turn, could lead to additional economic inefficiencies at the expense of small and medium-size enterprises that would suffer proportionately more in periods of economic distress. The result would be more economic and financial concentration.

Another question that needs to be addressed is whether financial institutions should experience the benefits and discomforts of monetary policy or should be mere conduits that pass the full impact of policy on to households and businesses. In the past two decades, financial institutions have increasingly become conduits. Through spread banking and other techniques, for example, they have quickly passed on the higher cost of funds to local government, business, and household borrowers in order to protect their own profit margins. As a result, much higher interest rates have been required to achieve effective monetary restraint.

The final demanders of credit—such as consumers, businesses, and governments—have been encumbered with a higher interest cost structure. The ability of financial institutions to shift higher costs quickly has encouraged them to become more entrepreneurial and more aggressive as merchandisers of credit. Similarly, the securitization of credit obligations is probably loosening the traditional ties between creditor and debtor, adding to the entrepreneurial drive in the financial system.

The disquieting manifestations of this financial entrepreneurship abound today. Despite a sharp deterioration in the quality of credit reflected on the balance sheets of financial institutions, the drive to exploit growth through the continuing rapid creation of debt is very much alive. Banking institutions that are overloaded with the debt of financially weak developing countries are currently striving to extend credit to sectors in which debtors are still viable, such as households and businesses.

The open credit market operates under the false assumption that marketability means high liquidity; it is exploiting the issuance of high-yield bonds and is taking on activities that are akin to bank lending practices. Financial market participants, however, will not escape from what has come about. The rapid growth of debt and its costs create a burden on households and businesses that is then, in turn, reflected back on the weaker and more marginal assets of our financial institutions; these institutions then become encumbered with inadequate capital and, consequently, experience pressures to improve profits by moving into other ventures. There is little solace when the deed has been done. By then, the financial system and its participants have been weakened.

In this context, the central bank operates precariously. It has to drive interest rates to hitherto unthinkably high levels when monetary policy restraint is required, because institutions have no vested interest in slowing credit availability early; it must also cut interest rates sharply once restraint is effective to avoid bankruptcies. The risk under this approach is that the central bank has to take on the role, increasingly, of lender of last resort to a wider range of financial and business participants. In essence, the recent changes in our financial system have facilitated the transfer of risk to the ultimate borrowers and investors. However, this has not eliminated risks from the system. Indeed, the process has contributed to a faster rate of debt creation, ultimately increasing the risks in the economy.

Financial institutions are not just the guardians of credit, but in a broader sense they are also the mechanisms that can either strengthen or weaken a market-based society. Financial institutions should be part of a process that encourages moderate growth of debt and substantial growth of equity and ownership. To be sure, to achieve such objectives, a correct fiscal and tax structure must be in place. Substantial risk taking and entrepreneurial zeal belong properly in the world of commerce and trade, where large equity capital tends to reside, and not in financial institutions that are heavily endowed with other people's money. Encouraging increased leveraging of financial institutions automatically induces greater leverage in the private sector, making this area more vulnerable and more marginal and eventually inviting government intervention. The whole process thus undermines the essence of an economic democracy.

In this regard, there are a number of unalterable facts. First, when financial institutions act with excessive entrepreneurial zeal, the immediate outcome is a contribution to economic and financial exhilaration. Only later, when the loan cannot be repaid on time or the investment turns sour, are the debilitating and restrictive aspects of the excesses fully evident. In addition, official exhortations to limit the excesses of financial entrepreneurship are inadequate if not futile.

To some extent, our current regulations encourage risk taking, because large institutions are not allowed to fail, and it is virtually impossible for major financial participants to remain uncompromised to some extent. As is clearly evident all about us today, the competitive pressure to be in the new mainstream of markets is intense. Growth aspirations are difficult to thwart once institutions set targets for profits, market penetration, and balance sheet size within a financial framework that prescribes no effective limits and that encourages, with great intensity, the application of financial ingenuity and liberal practices.

Thus, this issue comes down to whether financial institutions should be a vehicle for sheltering households and businesses from becoming highly exposed financially. I believe that a bias in this more prudent direction would be quite desirable. In addition to the vulnerabilities that I have already mentioned, a less entrepreneurial financial system would reduce the wide gyrations in the financial markets, encourage longer-term investment decisions, and focus society's efforts on meeting economic goals. As I will indicate later, this shift in financial direction is not yet beyond our reach.

Much of the debate on the reregulation versus the deregulation of financial institutions rests on just these issues. Do financial institutions serve an important public role, and in this role should financial institutions protect households and businesses from financial excesses? The debate should not be decided solely on the basis of the so-called inequities in the marketplace today or on the premise that U.S. financial institutions should have sufficient flexibility to compete with rapidly growing financial institutions and markets in the United States and abroad. The resolution of the debate on these particular points will not necessarily strengthen our system. What others do may not be right. Indeed, if our banks had been inhibited in the past from competing so aggressively in the international arena, they would be stronger—not weaker—organizations.

However, if the Congress decides that a more deregulated financial system is preferred, at least two challenges will have to be met: How are institutions and markets to be disciplined? And how will institutions have to be structured to compete on a level playing field? The disciplines of a deregulated financial system are simple in concept but difficult—if not impossible—in reality to accept, especially in a highly advanced economic society. Efficient institutions will amass profits and prosper, and inefficient ones will stumble and then fail.

The difficulty in accepting such disciplines reflects the fact that the failure of financial institutions involves other people's savings, along with temporary funds from the institutions in question and from other organizations linked to the financial institutions through the intermediation process. Moreover, such a deregulated system will surely burden households and businesses with an even greater overload of debt and make the economy more marginal. I hope that Congress will not move in this direction.

The obstacles to achieving a level playing field—a framework that would ensure competitive equality among the different types of institutions—are formidable. What kind of standards, if any, should institutions be required to adhere to? Can there be true competitive equality if the liabilities of some institutions are federally insured, while others are not? I doubt that deposit insurance can be eliminated from our financial system. If it were, market participants would assume that the official safety net would cover an even larger portfolio of the financial system until a major institution is allowed to fail, and then the risks of contraction in the financial system and economy would be extremely high. It is the type of risk that we, as a society, should avoid.

Now, much was said in the last two days of our discussions about the role of the commercial banks and the broader powers that should be accorded to them. However, in restructuring the financial system, we cannot overlook the many changes that have occurred in the open credit market, both here and abroad. Robert Eisenbeis spoke about the changes in clearing arrangements. On the whole, very little was said about the huge growth in open market transactions, in derivative credit instruments, in the credit exposures in the various clearing mechanisms, in the potential settlement problems, and in the extraordinary capacity to speculate in this financial world as compared with the more limited aggressive financial activity of a few decades ago.

In formulating the groundwork for an improved financial system, we cannot and should not return to the compartmentalized structure that prevailed years ago. Financial life is evolving, and we should be able to retain the best and discard undesirable aspects of this process of change. To ignore the developments in our financial world will invite the risk of substantial disarray. Those who favor further substantial deregulation do so on the grounds that such a system, by being highly competitive, will provide services at the lowest cost. They ignore both the special fiduciary role of institutions and the fact that the costs of service delivery are only one aspect in judging the performance of the financial system. They also fail to recognize the consequences of allowing failures to be the sole disciplining force in this system.

Advocates of substantial deregulation, however, do not agree when it comes to deposit insurance. Large institutions often favor the removal of insurance altogether or the setting of insurance fees associated with the risks involved in the insured institution. The assumption here is that large institutions will have an advantage, because even in a fully deregulated environment, the government would be much more hesitant to allow such institutions to fail. The likely consequence would be increased financial concentration. Deposit insurance based on the associated risks would probably also not work well, because higher fees would boost the costs of already marginal institutions, promote enlarged risk taking to offset these costs, and put depositors clearly on notice that they are maintaining accounts with a vulnerable institution where deposit insurance may not hold.

Many advocates of regulation want to maintain the status quo. This position, I believe, is completely unrealistic. Adherents to this view fail to acknowledge some of the important changes that I mentioned earlier: the aggressive bidding for funds by institutions, the globalization and securitization of markets, and the quick pass-through of costs by institutions to final demanders of credit. Only a few have called for some sort of new regulation. For example, E. Gerald Corrigan, president of the Federal Reserve Bank of New York, has put forth a well-reasoned and articulate set of proposals for reforming the financial structure. On the whole, he emphasizes arranging the institutions in our system into three groups: bank and thrift holding companies, financial holding companies, and commercial and financial conglomerates. I believe that this arrangement is influenced by his central banking responsibility. He wants to ensure that the central bank, as the lender of last resort, can function effectively in crisis periods.

Corrigan's analysis stresses having a well-functioning payments system, and he has argued persuasively for keeping commerce separate from banking. But as I stated earlier, the blurring of the distinction between money and credit means that safeguarding the payments mechanism is only one part of an improved financial regulatory structure.

What then should be done to establish a reformed financial system that recognizes the changes that have occurred and concurrently supplies the underpinnings to encourage stable economic growth and provide for the general well-being of an economic democracy? I suggest the following.

First, an official central authority should be established to oversee all major financial institutions and markets. Today, we live in a highly integrated financial system in which, as I noted earlier, institutions bid for funds and, in some instances, carry on comparable activities in the allocation of these funds. The current system of diverse and overlapping official supervision lacks a coherent overview and fails to meet the realities of the financial world today. This new central authority should also establish minimum capital requirements and uniform reporting standards, and it should require much greater disclosure of the profitability and balance sheet data of our institutions. When monetary restraint is required, this new centralized authority should increase the minimum capital of financial institutions. In this way, institutions would be restrained, and households and businesses would be less encumbered financially. The reverse would, of course, hold when monetary ease is needed. Capital requirements based on the riskiness of assets is a step in the right direction. This authority should also set a time schedule that would require all institutions to report their asset values at the lower of cost or market. Such a requirement would further inhibit the weakening of our financial institutions.

Second, an official international authority should be established to oversee major financial institutions and markets, regardless of their locations. Its membership should consist of representatives from the major industrial nations. As noted earlier, global financial institutions and markets exist today—a fact that makes the supervision of institutions and markets by national authorities ineffective. Borrowers and institutions quickly arbitrage the regulatory capital requirements and other differences between one financial center and another. At times, the agility of market participants limits the policy effectiveness of central banks. Consider, for example, how easy it is for participants who have access to international financial markets to circumvent the policy objectives of central banks or how much more forcefully others have to be constrained in order for monetary policy restraint to achieve its objective in tightening markets. Such an official international authority should set minimum capital and reporting standards for all major institutions that operate internationally, and uniform trading practices and standards should be established for participants in open market activities.

Third, because conflicts of interest run the serious risk of undermining the efficient functioning of the financial system and the economy, they must be avoided. There are three activities that need to be kept apart: lending, underwriting of securities, and equity investing. Conflicts of interest are bound to arise if these activities are joined.

With these conflicts of interest in mind, the following principles should underlie new financial regulations.

First, commercial and financial institutions belong apart. Second, financial institutions should not be allowed to be both lenders and equity investors. The system of regulation should force financial institutions in their dealings with the business sector to choose whether to be an underwriter, a lender, or an equity investor. Finally, deposit insurance should be used to strengthen the financial system—and not serve only as a guarantee of the safety of deposits. The proceeds from all insured deposits should be required to be invested either in high-grade securities or in loans that the official regulators deem to be highly creditworthy. If deposit institutions prefer to make lower-quality loans and investments, they should be booked in another institution and financed with noninsured funds.

There are no easy and quick solutions to the problems that now permeate our financial system. Policy makers should focus not on how quickly the last vestiges of the Glass-Steagall Act can be removed, but rather on the question: "If not Glass-Steagall, then what?" A fully deregulated financial system is not the solution. Financial institutions have a unique public responsibility. Consequently, a better-regulated financial system that incorporates the many changes that have taken place in the past few decades is, in my opinion, the correct way. This will position financial institutions and markets to facilitate economic growth instead of contributing to substantial economic turbulence in the future.

# 5

# *Debt: The Threat to Economic and Financial Stability*

*The financial community—indeed, the world—now recognizes the out-of-control growth of debt (especially poor-quality debt) as a central cause of economic weakness and financial crisis. I began to highlight the troubling trend beginning in the late 1960s, and assessed the growing risks in this 1986 talk at the well-known annual gathering of leading economists and policy makers in Jackson Hole, Wyoming.*

It was in the late 1960s when I first detected that developments in debt creation might be taking an ominous turn. Since then I have spoken about the subject a number of times. While many debt problems have surfaced in recent years, the issue of debt and financial stability does not yet have the national attention that it so crucially deserves. Now, the problems associated with debt are well past their infancy and, indeed, are dangerously full-grown. Even so, there is still only some awareness today that debt has both a sunny and a dark side to it. Historically, the act of creating debt contributed to economic and financial exhilaration. But in the past several years, we have realized that the obligations inherent in debt may impose hardships on lenders and borrowers and, indeed, on the economy and the financial markets as a whole.

The reality is that our debt problem is not going to go away. It is complex; there are no easy solutions. To cope successfully with this problem and to stave off an economic disruption of major proportions, the role of our financial system will need to be redefined, and structural changes and disciplines that are lacking today will have to be imposed. Unfortunately, there is as yet no evidence that adequate measures will be undertaken soon to ameliorate this situation.

Debt expansion is also outrunning nominal gross national product (GNP) growth. Credit market debt outstanding at the end of 1985 exceeded nominal GNP by a ratio of 2:1. In 1980, debt was 70 percent higher than GNP, and in both 1960 and 1970, it was roughly 50 percent higher than GNP.

All major sectors of the economy have accelerated their use of credit. Corporate debt, for example, increased by 12.4 percent in 1985, compared with 9.4 percent annually in the 1960s. Household debt rose by 12.8 percent in 1985, up from an annual average increase of 8.6 percent in the 1960s. But the most dramatic step-up by far in borrowings has been incurred by governments: U.S. government debt rose at an annual rate of 2 percent in the 1960s and by 9 percent in the 1970s, and has soared by almost 16 percent annually thus far in the 1980s. Concurrently, state and local government debt expanded by around 7.5 percent annually in the 1960s and 1970s and has jumped to 12.5 percent per year thus far in the 1980s. Debt has also burgeoned internationally. At the end of 1985, the medium- and long-term external debt of less developed countries totaled $781 billion, or 159 percent of their gross merchandise exports, compared with $173 billion, or 73 percent of their merchandise exports, in 1975.

A significant deterioration in the quality of credit has accompanied this swift debt growth. In the United States, this has been most noticeable in the business sector, where more credit ratings have been downgraded than upgraded since the start of the current business expansion in 1982. Today, the universe of AAA-rated industrial and utility corporations has been cut to 26 from 56 a decade ago, when the economy was smaller. Currently, the size of the high-yield bond market (with credit ratings below BBB) is about $100 billion, or roughly 21 percent of outstanding corporate bonds. In 1976, the size of this market was nearly $19 billion, or 9 percent of outstanding bonds. At present, only the paper of one large bank holding company is rated AAA. Ten years ago, this numbered 14. This credit quality deterioration is also evident in other sectors. In the state and local government market, overall credit quality eroded for the seventh consecutive year in 1985, the latest year for which we have complete data. In the agricultural sector, the value of farmland, after peaking in 1981, has fallen by 25 percent, while farm debt has continued to mount. As a result, over the past five years, farmers' net worth has fallen by 30 percent, and many farms are in financial disrepair. Even households do not show the financial strength that they enjoyed a decade ago.

Both the ratios of household debt to disposable personal income and to net worth are at record highs—they were 25 percent and 15 percent lower, respectively, 10 years ago (1976). In the current business expansion, the consumer's appetite for credit has been voracious. In the past four years, for example, while disposable income has risen by 32 percent, households have taken on 42 percent more in mortgage debt and an extraordinary 73 percent more in installment debt.

In addition to the ongoing deterioration in these sectors of the economy, there is a relatively new area of weakness—commercial real estate construction. We are just beginning to realize the extent of this problem. Significant real estate loan losses have been reported at a number of large banking and thrift institutions, not only in the Southwest,

## Jackson Hole Refrain

Sixteen years after I delivered this talk at the famed Jackson Hole conference, I was still trying to bring attention to the role of monetary officials in reining in debt. I made the following comment at the August 2002 Jackson Hole conference, "Rethinking Stabilization Policy."

We have just ended or are in the middle of the largest bubble in the post–World War II period. Probably combining Japan and the United States, we haven't seen anything like this since the 1920s. Nevertheless, in our discussions here, we more or less come to the conclusion that there is very little that monetary policy can do to address this kind of an issue, to mitigate it, and so on. That is disturbing, considering what has happened. We have seen a huge increase in debt outstandings. We have seen a massive deterioration in corporate credit quality. We have seen household participation in open-credit market instruments that is unprecedented as such. And the speed with which money flows back and forth and across borders is unprecedented, certainly in the post–World War II period. There is also the issue of what the role of a central bank is—perhaps not for all central banks—in the supervision of financial institutions. The failure of effective supervision contributed to the bubbling. We haven't discussed this.

Finally, there is another aspect we used to hear about when it came to monetary policy in the past. What is the role of moral suasion? What should central bankers be saying at appropriate times to really try to reverse attitudes and procedures, particularly if the statements that were made here [are correct] that central bankers are highly popular? If they are highly popular, they would be listened to. If so, moral suasion should be utilized.

Excerpted from "Rethinking Stabilization Policy," a symposium sponsored by the Federal Reserve Bank of Kansas City, Jackson Hole, Wyoming, August 29-31, 2002.

but nationwide, reflecting the fact that rental income is insufficient to support the debt service of many office projects.

An additional facet of the debt problem concerns the data. Now, all of us who have worked with debt data should readily concede the shortcomings of these statistics. The Federal Reserve's flow-of-funds data, a prime source for many of us, have many flaws. For example, information on state and local government borrowing is provided with a long time lag by the Census Department. The U.S. Treasury, for cost-cutting reasons, has moved to voluntary reporting on many of the capital flows between residents of the United States and foreigners. The data on borrowing and investing abroad by domestic corporations are inadequate in terms of accuracy, completeness, and timeliness. The statistics on corporate pension funds and public retirement funds are incomplete and, like many other data, are available only with a considerable delay.

Nevertheless, imperfections in the data do not invalidate the conclusion that the nation faces a very serious debt problem. If anything, the available data probably understate the magnitude of the problem. For example, the Federal Reserve's flow-of-funds data tend to be revised sharply upward from the preliminary report. Two years after the release of the preliminary fourth-quarter 1983 flow-of-funds statistics, the upward revision for nonfinancial debt was nearly 7 percent. It ranged as high as 40 percent for some subsectors.

In addition, we should all understand that the enormity of the debt situation is being masked by accounting conventions and liberal official regulatory standards. Financial statements often tend to show a netting out of assets and liabilities. Given current balance sheet conventions, many business and financial entities probably employ greater leverage of debt to capital than is readily discernible.

How did this enormous growth of debt come about, and what is sustaining it? Merely to blame the incorrect policies that fueled inflation is too easy; there is much more to the debt explosion. I have written at length about the underlying causes of the surge in debt. For this discussion, let me summarize with the following seven points: the attitude toward debt, financial deregulation, financial innovation, securitization, financial internationalization, the tax structure, and practicing debt prudence.

1. **The attitude toward debt** has been transformed from a hesitancy to borrow in the early post–World War II period to an intense use of credit in recent years. This attitudinal change reflects the declining influence of those who experienced the Great Depression of the 1930s. Indeed, despite a number of significant financial crises during the past 20 years, only relatively few institutions failed. Today, no one celebrates paying off the home mortgage. Now, corporate financing strategies do not differentiate between money and credit or between liabilities and liquidity.

2. **Financial deregulation**, regardless of its merits, still facilitates the creation of debt, because it spurs competition and reinforces the drive for new markets and enlarged market standing. Credit growth was more inhibited when markets were more compartmentalized and institutions were more restricted in their activities.

3. **Financial innovation**, by its very nature, either facilitates borrowing that could not have been financed at all using earlier techniques or is utilized to reduce financing costs. Perhaps the most far-reaching of the many changes that have been introduced in the past few decades has been floating-rate financing. This technique enables financial institutions to try to insulate themselves from the interest rate risk by quickly passing on increases in the cost of their sources of funds to their borrowers. In the past, a move toward higher interest rates curbed debt growth because financial institutions could not easily pass on the higher costs to their customers. But with the advent of the pass-through device of the floating-rate note, financial

institutions have become aggressively more entrepreneurial and growth oriented than in the past.

4. **Securitization,** which transforms obligations from nonmarketable to marketable, has encouraged debt growth in several ways. First, it tends to create the illusion that credit risk can be reduced if the credit instruments become marketable. Holders of the marketable obligation frequently believe that they have the foresight to sell before the decrease in creditworthiness is perceived by the market. Second, the enhancement techniques employed in securitization, such as credit guarantees and insurance, blur the credit risk and raise the vexing question, "Who is the real guardian of credit?"

5. **Internationalization of finance** has also enhanced debt creation. Today, major corporations and official and private institutions seek the best terms by borrowing in Europe, the United States, and Japan. Rapid advances in communications and technology, together with financial deregulation abroad, have intensified competition among key financial centers. In view of the differences in the degrees of deregulation, regulatory requirements, and accounting standards, the opportunity to generate debt is very great indeed.

6. **Our tax structure** is another factor that encourages the use of debt over equity. Interest payments are generally tax deductible. Although this preferential treatment may be curtailed somewhat by the proposed tax reform, dividend payments are still subject to double taxation, and the levy on capital gains may be raised.

7. **Practicing financial prudence** is virtually impossible for major participants in our financial system. Even the best compromise. For business corporations, this may happen through the use of greater leveraging in order to avoid a takeover. As I have noted in my book *Interest Rates, the Markets, and the New Financial World* (Times Books, 1986), "If (financial) participants fail to adapt to the new world of securitized debt, proxy debt instruments, and floating-rate financing,

then they lose market share, make only limited profits, and do not attract the most skilled people. The driving force behind profit generation is credit growth."

What risks does the mounting debt pose for financial stability? Here no simple formula will reveal to us the flashpoints of economic and financial trouble. The fact is that the debt buildup in the past two decades has been greater than most would have thought tolerable. Several credit crises have been surmounted, and both the economy and the financial markets have survived. Interest rates rose to levels that were unimaginable in earlier years. But, while the financial system remained intact, its structure and financial practices were altered dramatically. Nevertheless, it cannot be denied that our system is now more marginal and more highly leveraged than at any time in the past 40 years. This might be less disturbing if business cycle volatility had been curtailed, but this has not been the case. Another matter of concern is that debt can severely restrict freedom of action when income slows and debt servicing needs preempt much of the income that is left. In contrast, of course, large equity positions relative to debt provide society with enhanced freedom and with maximum economic flexibility. Given these observations, huge debt will add a very troubling dimension to the next business recession. If a major economic and financial upheaval is to be avoided, official policy makers must act with alacrity. There will be less leeway for errors in policy decisions and implementation.

The greatest need is to harness effectively the growth of debt. How can this be accomplished in our new financial world of deregulation, securitization, globalization, and innovation? We cannot and should not attempt to return to the financial markets of yesteryear. Too much has changed. We need a framework that will get the best out of the current financial system and ward off the worst. The resolution to the debt problem has at least two dimensions. One is immediate. How do we defuse the debt explosion without risking a major economic calamity? The other is closely related. It involves the kind of disciplines and practices that should be implemented to foster reasonable, but not excessive, debt growth.

Unfortunately, history offers little encouragement in this regard. In the period prior to World War II, excessive debt was generally eliminated through bankruptcies and failures, which, if large enough, brought about precipitous economic contractions. Today, this form of discipline has become unacceptable, although during each economic contraction in the postwar years, debt growth slowed but debt did not shrink. Actually, we are moving in a new direction in this new financial world of ours in which aggressive financial practices are proliferating. An official safety net is being spread under many financial activities. No longer are market forces allowed to exercise their full discipline over large financial institutions. Depositors of smaller institutions enjoy the protection of that safety net. It is also my belief that obligations covered by credit insurance and by the implied guarantee of the federal government—as is the case with many credit agencies—benefit from an implied official safety net.

With this in mind, how do we steer the economy toward moderate debt growth and at the same time avoid deflation? The magnitude of the debt problem itself suggests that it would seriously undermine the ability of the economy to revive quickly from the next business recession. Consequently, until there is solid evidence of a significant economic rebound, monetary policy must take the risk and err even further on the side of accommodation. Lower interest rates will ease the debt burden in the United States and, particularly, in developing countries. Further monetary ease will give many marginal borrowers the opportunity to survive. We must stretch out the period in which debts can be written off by creditors and in which debtors, therefore, can recoup earning power. To be sure, this monetary policy approach runs the risk of rekindling inflation, but the alternative—deflation—is also punishing and is the more immediate threat to our economic and financial stability.

On the one hand, the monetary throttle can always be pulled back if need be, but on the other hand, once a deflation is under way, even large reserve injections may not immediately halt the decline in economic activity and the contraction in income flows.

Monetary policy makers today face the dilemma that the new financial world has rendered obsolete the once-simple rules for conducting policy. In this new setting, the Federal Reserve is encumbered by a poorly defined monetary approach; therefore, it must be more highly judgmental than in the past. The Federal Reserve must have insights into the rapidly changing financial developments and their policy implications. Even if these insights are timely, they may not be sufficient in formulating an effective policy, because many of the new financial practices are beyond the immediate control of the Federal Reserve.

In addition to the immediate monetary policy quandary in dealing with the debt explosion, there is the serious question of appropriate fiscal policy. Since the U.S. government has accelerated the rate of its borrowings more than any other sector, it would seem at first blush that a sharp reduction in the budget deficit would be appropriate. Here, we face a serious judgment problem in policy, because a drastic pullback in the deficit would contribute to fiscal drag just when economic growth is seriously lacking vigor. This, in turn, will add to the Federal Reserve's difficulty in deciding how much more accommodating monetary policy should be in order to offset the fiscal drag. Some studies have claimed that fiscal policy initially can have a more powerful influence than monetary policy. A study by the Organization for Economic Cooperation and Development (OECD), for example, reveals that a two-percentage-point cut in short-term interest rates raises real GNP growth in the United States by half a percentage point over three years, while a rise in government spending by 1 percent of gross domestic product (GDP) increases the level of real GDP by 2½ percent during this period. Although this example may overstate the problem, if there is a fiscal pullback, then the pressure is on monetary policy to be very accommodating.

The fiscal quandary and its implications for debt growth and economic and financial stability are deeper still. A large reduction in the deficit over a short time span weakens economic activity even further, while small reductions would do little to solve the deficit problem. If another recession should take place with a large deficit at the outset, it will be extremely difficult for our legislators to quickly opt for an even higher deficit. Thus, the legacy of the debt explosion that we have experienced may well be that the next recession will have to be overcome mainly through monetary ease with little help from fiscal policy. University of St. Louis economist Hyman Minsky has often pointed out that fiscal and monetary stimulus has rescued the financial system from the crises since World War II. The question for the future is: Can monetary policy do it alone the next time around?

Much of the feared reflation that might result from substantial monetary stimulation over the near term would most likely be contained if we initiate structures and disciplines that are rooted in the realities of the new financial world. Procedures and a governing process should be set up that fully recognize that markets and institutions are no longer neatly compartmentalized. I continue to believe that the following eight suggestions, if adopted, would go a long way toward stabilizing the debt situation.

1. Many of the current regulatory bodies should be eliminated. In our rapidly changing financial system, in which institutions perform a multiplicity of services, is it efficient to have so many regulators on both the state and federal levels? These regulators are largely vestiges of our past financial development. At times, they compete with each other, and they do not have an integrated view of today's financial world.
2. Centralized monitoring and regulation of our financial system should be established. I continue to urge, as I did in congressional

testimony more than a year ago, that the prudential responsibilities of the Federal Reserve should be enlarged to encompass institutions other than banks, or that a National Board of Overseers should be established that would monitor and promulgate codes of minimum behavior for all major financial institutions.

3. Financial institutions should be required to report their assets at the lower of cost or market value. Losses would then be quickly recorded, inducing managers of financial institutions to turn toward more conservative practices.

4. There should be much greater disclosure by financial market participants—including institutions and corporations—in their financial statements. Assets and liabilities should not be netted out. Contingent liabilities should be reported in detail, thus providing creditors with the opportunity to improve their ability to assess the credit standing of debtors.

5. If this type of disclosure continues to be inadequate, then the official regulatory agencies should be required to rate the creditworthiness of the financial institutions under their jurisdiction. These ratings should be made public after a delay, thereby allowing the institutions time to remedy any problems before the public is apprised.

6. We should adopt tax policies that foster the enlargement of equity capital, rather than the excessive use of debt. In this regard, the double taxation of dividends and the capital gains tax on equity shares should be eliminated.

7. The official regulatory agencies should issue regulations that require the gradual enlargement of the capital base of the institutions under their supervision.

8. To contain the debt problem, international cooperation and coordination must be strengthened. A new official international organization, consisting of key central banks and other officials, should be established. This organization should work toward achieving uniform accounting, capital, and reporting standards of major financial institutions. It should monitor more closely international capital

flows by promulgating better reporting standards. In a world with a rapidly growing web of financial linkages, such improvements are essential not only to rein in debt growth, but also to achieve effective monetary policies.

These recommendations are designed not so that we return to the structural world of finance of a few decades ago, but rather to remedy the problems that have been created in this new environment. If failures and bankruptcies are unacceptable, then institutions and markets must be required to adhere to standards that prevent many of them from moving to the brink of failure. A strong financial system should encourage equity instead of debt and should insist on understated asset values rather than liberal accounting standards and hidden liabilities. The changes that need to be made to prevent a debt crisis from causing major damage are difficult to engineer, because the many vested interests involved will attempt to limit the necessary legislative initiatives. The urgent need is for far-reaching decisions now—not when the debt problem has completely overwhelmed us.

# 6

# *The Decapitalization of American Corporations*

*One of the most damaging and least understood dimensions of the exploding debt crisis (see previous chapter) is the massive shift of corporate finance away from equity toward debt. In this talk at the National Press Club in 1989, I zeroed in on the specific dimensions, implications, and possible remedies of the troubling trend—a trend that has only accelerated since this cautionary speech.*

For many years now, a disturbing disregard for capital has been permeating some important segments of American business and threatening our nation's economic well-being. This disregard is not limited to the corporate sector. There are other manifestations. It is present in the exorbitant demand for credit on the part of the federal government that results from an inability to make necessary budgetary reductions. It is also seen in a continuing rise of personal indebtedness by the household sector.

One especially worrisome trends is the prolonged, and highly undesirable, shift away from equity toward debt financing by many business corporations. This shift has accelerated in recent years as a result of the corporate merger and acquisition (M&A) and leveraged buyout (LBO) mania, which, in a number of ways, has heightened the disregard for capital. I believe that unless something is done to forestall excesses that are almost inevitable in this area, the health of the free enterprise system in the United States will be endangered.

To some, this may seem to overstate the menace. But the merger, acquisition, and leveraged buyout mania poses significant hazards for a number of reasons:

- **First**, it creates a real threat to the financial viability of the corporations involved. That threat will become harshly apparent to everyone in the next recession, whenever that may come.
- **Second**, it serves to undermine the basic strength of the stock market. In the short term, it distorts normal trading activity as market participants become increasingly obsessed with uncovering where the next deal will come from. For the longer term, it erodes investor confidence in the underlying fairness of the markets. And from a cyclical perspective, the exaggerated dependence of the market on mergers, acquisitions, and buyouts will end up contributing to a sharper decline in share values when the next recession draws nearer.
- **Third**, it does permanent damage to the corporate bond market. As a result, the cost of long-term debt financing will rise for all business organizations, even those not directly involved in M&As or LBOs themselves. And that will encourage still shorter-maturity financing to escape the high cost of long-term funds, aggravating corporate financial vulnerability.
- **Fourth**, it weakens the competitive position of U.S. business internationally. That is because over a period of time the large increases in leverage and debt servicing that accompany corporate financial restructurings will make it more difficult for many U.S. firms to embark on essential investment projects. But corporations in the other major industrial countries are improving their balance sheet positions—and hence their capacity to finance productive investments and sustain their competitive strength.
- **Fifth**, it decreases our government's revenue and thus increases the budget deficit.

Now, I would not go so far as to assert that all highly leveraged corporate restructurings are unwise. Some may well yield positive economic effects. But taken too far, the decapitalization of American corporations will cause future financial stress. Ultimately, it will put the government into the business of business through bailouts that will move our system closer to a social democracy and away from an economic democracy.

This variant of socialization probably will not happen suddenly, as the outcome of some dramatic shock. Instead, the pathology of excessive leverage is to infect the system slowly, with few immediate overt symptoms of financial disease. But once under way, the infection is virtually impossible to reverse. It will cause profound changes in the system, amounting to a major upheaval in our economic and financial way of life. Excessive leveraging will encourage a growing concentration of assets and of decision making in the private sector.

Out of that will emerge a financial-industrial complex wherein financial institutions and industrial corporations become increasingly interwoven, rather than separate and distinct entities. That amalgam will invite various forms of governmental intrusion, culminating in direct government participation in business through bailouts of corporations that fall into severe financial difficulties.

But for now, and possibly for some time to come, these long-term adverse consequences for the country will be either ignored or dismissed. Unfortunately, the immediate financial rewards to the participants in the game are so large and tempting that a whole series of self-justifications have come forth in favor of these deals. Thus, more and bigger deals will continue to be pursued until either there is a major failure or until government steps in to check the excesses that will inevitably occur at some point.

There is no clear consensus on why precisely the M&A and LBO mania is happening right now, whether it is an indictment of a generation of ineffective management; an incorrectly structured tax system; a natural result of loose, abundant credit; or an outgrowth of our weakened international financial position. Doubtless, many factors are responsible. But there is no dispute that it is contributing to a decapitalization of U.S. business that is progressing at a rampant pace.

It entails a staggering substitution of new debt for outstanding equity. Over the past five years the debt of U.S. nonfinancial corporations has gone up by an estimated $840 billion and the equity position has contracted by nearly $300 billion.

In the latest economic expansion, nonfinancial corporate debt has grown by 15.4 percent annually, compared with an annual increase of only 8.4 percent for the previous six cyclical periods of economic growth.

In the process, interest payments by U.S. nonfinancial corporations have swelled to a point where they now amount to about 26 percent of internal cash flow. To put this number in perspective, these payments now preempt more internal cash flow than during the *recessions* of 1982 and 1974, when this ratio was 22 percent and 19 percent, respectively.

One price of this leveraging explosion is a severe drop in credit quality. Nineteen eighty-eight was the seventh consecutive year in which there were more downgradings in ratings by the major credit services than upgradings. As a result, only a handful of major corporations are still rated AAA, and the number of companies rated A and AA is also dwindling.

Some claim that the merger, acquisition, and leveraged buyout activity imposes limited systemic risks as long as it involves noncyclical businesses, those that presumably produce a steady cash flow. This is a substantial overstatement of the facts. Even noncyclical businesses are adversely affected by downturns in economic activity, though not as much as heavy industries.

In this connection, the new dimensions of the interaction between monetary restraint and its impact on economic participants are not taken into consideration. In our new deregulated financial world, for the central bank to achieve effective restraint, it must force a denial of credit at a much higher level of interest rates than when markets were more segmented. Monetary restraint is successful only after considerable scrambling for credit takes place among businesses, households, and government. Thus, many so-called noncyclical businesses will become more bruised than heretofore, including consumer goods, retailing, and service industries.

Moreover, the so-called cyclical sector has not been a small proportion of the merger and leveraged buyout activity. According to a recent study by Goldman Sachs, corporations in cyclical industries accounted for nearly $200 billion or 40 percent of merger and acquisition activity and for $35 billion or again 40 percent of the leveraged buyouts since 1982.

What is important to bear in mind is that this decapitalization of so much of American industry has come into vogue under relatively benign economic conditions. The weakened financial structure of many corporations has not been tested during a business contraction. When it comes, there will not be the swollen sales, revenues, and corporate income readily available to service a bloated mass of debt that there is today. Consequently, the chances are high that companies with a highly leveraged capital structure will report losses that are much larger than normal in a cyclical economic downturn. For quite a few, cash flow will be inadequate to service debt. For many, there will need to be various kinds of reschedulings and workouts to avoid bankruptcy proceedings.

By then, the issue will be raised in a political context of whether the nation is prepared to accept the full discipline of the marketplace to exorcise these excesses of leverage. Will firms that took on massive amounts of debt be allowed to fail, even if that would threaten to worsen the business contraction? Or will there be a clamor for a safety net, a lender of last resort in the form of a governmental bailout? After all, many who are now perpetuating the M&A and LBO mania will be suffering acutely—lenders with fiduciary responsibilities, banks, pension funds, and insurance companies.

For the Federal Reserve, the dilemma of how to conduct monetary policy during the next recession for an economy laden with heavily indebted corporations will be especially acute. We have to ask: To what extent will our central bank have to accelerate monetary ease to avoid an immediate financial calamity—even if that means prematurely reigniting inflation and seriously damaging the prospects for a noninflationary recovery? And, if the central bank routinely accommodates the bailouts, will it not end up being little more than an accomplice in encouraging the drift toward a socialization of economic and financial activity?

The international consequences of the explosion of corporate debt are no less worrisome. Just at a time when this nation is trying to regain international competitiveness so that we can improve our trade position, the additional debt burdens on many companies will have a crippling effect. In contrast, financial positions of major corporations abroad are getting stronger. In Japan, for instance, large increases in retained earnings have lowered corporate debt-to-equity ratios by some 10 percent in the past two years. A general pattern of improving equity positions is common throughout Europe as well.

The proponents of an uninhibited market in corporate control, those who applaud the M&A and LBO mania, dismiss these concerns. Debt poses no burdens, they contend; if economic adversity ensues, debt is easily restructured. Leverage ratios are of little concern; companies in Europe and Japan have long had higher debt-to-equity ratios without adverse consequences. Monetary policy need not be influenced by corporate debt; it merely substitutes for debt that would otherwise have been accumulated by the household sector. And, the proponents assert, managers of companies will find it easier to pursue long-term strategies when they don't have to be subservient to the short-term time horizons of people in the stock market.

I find these assertions unconvincing. High levels of debt create fragility and a far greater vulnerability to economic shocks—unless society is willing to go along with the kind of close, even intrusive, banking and government involvement in industry that is institutionally embedded in countries such as Germany and Japan. But for our institutional setting, there is ample historical evidence supporting the financial dictum that a large equity position allows corporations to assume greater risks and to pursue opportunities that debt-heavy corporations must forgo. Moreover, I know of no groups of shareholders who today are standing in the way of the management of a publicly traded corporation moving to improve the long-term efficiency of the firm. Shareholders do not resist these efforts; they yearn for them.

To argue that companies without shareholders but with huge amounts of debt somehow have more flexibility to achieve positive change in a business strikes me as both disingenuous and historically inaccurate.

Nevertheless, the unfortunate truth is that nearly all parties involved in the M&A and LBO mania have a strong vested interest in its continuation.

- Existing members of management normally have stock options that can be cashed out at high premiums. Plus in a management buyout, they get substantial portions of the equity in the new entity on which further profits can be recorded.
- Most stockholders are passive and enjoy the instant gratification of the high premiums paid by the bidders, and then take their money elsewhere.
- Commercial bankers get high fees for organizing and participating in the loan syndications. They get substantial interest rate spreads over the prime lending rate. In this day and age, when competition for credits is extremely fierce, these deals are nearly irresistible for the banks, regardless of the risks involved.
- Investment bankers and lawyers get high fees as advisers, so lucrative that it is very difficult for them to be objective in identifying the negative aspects of the deals they are pushing.

- In many instances, the investment bankers also stand to benefit twice over as underwriters and as sellers of debt securities in the public markets that are usually required to pay down the bridge loans, part of which are domiciled on the investment bankers' own books.

About the only stakeholder that is plainly an instant loser is the holder of the existing bonds of the company. Frankly, the bondholders do not have a strong enough constituency to get themselves bailed out or a clear enough legal standing to prevail in the courtroom for financial damages.

The class of instant beneficiaries also includes the equity market at large. To the extent that shares are withdrawn, that tends to make market prices elsewhere higher than they would be otherwise. In addition, the M&A and LBO mania sets off a scramble to find the next potential candidates to go through the process, and their share prices are bid up substantially. In fact, a large part of the strength in the U.S. equity market today can be traced to the phenomenon. Other, more stable sources of demand for stock have largely retreated from the market, especially pension funds and individual investors with long-term horizons. The scent of the deal and the short-term killing that can be made in anticipating the next LBO or M&A have replaced other considerations. What it means is that for the time being the equity markets have almost become addicted, and any measures aimed at slowing down the tempo of M&A and LBO activity is bound to weaken the prices of equity in general.

In view of this relatively new behavior of management, investors, and financial institutions, it is appropriate to ask, "Who are the guardians of capital?" It had been generally believed that it was business and investors who naturally exercised that responsibility. Much seems to have changed. The role of the powerful large individual stockholder-manager has diminished. New stockholder groups have frequently avoided a participatory evaluation of management. In most instances, the important new class of stockholders—institutional investors—tends to sell their shares rather than question management decisions. Moreover, the institutional portfolio practices of our day stress modern portfolio theory and equity risk diversification, not stockholder-management involvement. As a result, corporate managers are often independent trustees of a sort for a silent and absentee stockholder group.

The role of the institutional lenders, such as banks, has also shifted away from being the defender of capital to being financial entrepreneurs. They frequently resist the call for higher prudential capital ratios and more conservative accounting standards. Government-insured deposits, a technique for obtaining low-cost funds, have financed all sorts of marginal lending in an attempt to capture large profits.

Isn't it rather startling to find that before the loan problems of the Less Developed Countries and of the thrift institutions have been put to rest, the financial markets are enveloped in another speculative financing binge? Yet, the way our current world of institutions and markets is now structured, they cannot avoid being caught up in the creation of marginal debt. Today, even the most conservative institutions compromise standards and engage in practices that they would not have cared to pursue a decade or two ago. The heroes are the daring—those who are ready and willing to exploit leverage and risk the loss of credit standing to revel in the present casino-like atmosphere of the markets.

With the onslaught today of financial deregulation, innovation, and new technology, it is impossible for institutions and markets to be the defenders of capital. Consequently, it is the government, as the representative of all constituents, that must assume this urgent role.

We all must begin to appreciate that corporate debt can never be a full substitute for equity. Debt involves defined corporate obligations of interest payments and repayment schedules. It is a preemptive factor in corporate cash flow and may limit management flexibility.

The abuse of the debt-creation process contributes to corporate failures, and for society as a whole runs the risk of debauching the essence of economic democracy. Equity, in contrast, allows freedom of decision making and often reflects confidence in society and its political and economic institutions. If we diminish the role of equity, we invite the specter of business control first shifting to financial institutions and then inexorably toward government. In the process, we risk a social and political change away from freedom.

For its part, the government has two good reasons to respond promptly to the escalation of high leveraging within the corporate sector.

First is the straightforward adverse revenue effect on the U.S. Treasury. Decapitalization substitutes tax-deductible debt for equity, so over time corporate taxable income will be lower than it would be otherwise. To be sure, there are partial offsets. Some existing stock is held by people who pay capital gains taxes, and the lofty premiums paid by bidders will generate one-time capital gains collections. And some of the new junk bonds will be issued to taxpaying individuals and institutions. But over the long haul, the cumulative effect of an unchecked movement from equity to debt will permanently and substantially reduce corporate tax collections by tens of billions of dollars. Thus, the government is subsidizing decapitalization of U.S. industry.

Second, and probably more important, the government has to be concerned that the weakened financial structure of corporations effectively leaves the government with the implicit burden of having to come to the rescue of failed companies the next time the economy turns downward—or else risk a major national financial catastrophe.

If the market cannot discipline itself, then the government will have to consider ways of asserting the necessary discipline. It is no excuse to shy away from action on the assertion that no feasible set of restrictions will be perfect. Of course not. But just because what can be done will be imperfect doesn't mean nothing should be done.

I have a few suggestions for consideration. They are not meant to be exhaustive; many other proposals have merit and deserve to be considered. Here is my list:

- **First**, the government needs to reconsider the double taxation of dividends, a prime reason why many companies prefer debt over equity. Other countries have faced this problem and have developed reasonable compromises to eliminate or greatly reduce the imbalance in tax treatment. It is time our government did so as well.
- **Second**, there needs to be a review of capital gains taxation. Modifications ought to be made to raise the tax rate on short-term gains and eliminate it, or lower it substantially, for various classes of longer-term gains.
- **Third**, the capital requirements of financial institutions providing the financing for these deals should be scrutinized more closely. Any system of risk-based capital standards ought to treat especially strictly deals that involve huge quantities of debt and that depend heavily on locating eager buyers to purchase the subsidiaries that the borrowing company intends to spin off to help repay the bank loans.
- **Fourth**, beyond the formal application of impersonal numerical ratios, the central bank ought to be involved at the personal level with bank management, playing a leadership role in pressing for a return to conservative banking principles that are all too often neglected in the quest for quick profits. To take one practical illustration, that should involve insisting that syndicators of LBO loans accept a continuing responsibility toward the institutions to which they sell loans, even if a deal goes sour.

- **Fifth**, it is questionable whether any government-insured deposits should be allowed to be invested in these loans or in the junk bonds that are then issued to retire them. If banks and thrifts choose to participate, let it be in separate affiliates not funded by insured deposits.
- **Sixth**, securities firms should not be allowed to underwrite securities for firms in which they have a direct stake themselves, whether an equity stake or a bridge loan. Disclosure of such positions is insufficient as a check on potential abuses. How can an investment banking firm do objective due diligence for the securities to be distributed to the public when the proceeds of the offering will pay off the bridge loan lodged in the securities firms' own holdings?
- **Seventh**, bondholders in the existing securities of the firm should be given an explicit legal right to sue the organizers of an LBO or other corporate decapitalization for damages ensuing from the resulting downgrading of the credit ratings of those bonds caused by that restructuring.
- **Eighth**, whenever the management of a company makes a bid for its company, there should be an immediate inquiry as to whether the group is utilizing inside information not disclosed to shareholders. Plus, a written explanation should be published why the business plan that the group intends to adopt after the LBO cannot be pursued as a publicly held company.
- **Ninth**, sufficient time, perhaps 90 days, should be provided for other bidders to compete whenever members of existing management propose an LBO.
- **Tenth**, I do not favor measures that directly limit the participation of the foreign institutional lenders that have been extremely important in the financing of many merger transactions. They should, however, exercise some restraint. Regulatory authorities of the United States and other major countries have already made progress in developing uniform capital standards for banks. It would make sense to extend these efforts to include explicitly the treatment of merger financing. Moreover, I doubt that any major industrial country would want to

be identified as a prominent source of funds facilitating the decapitalization of American enterprises. A continuing dialogue on this matter
between U.S. and foreign officials will go a long way in harmonizing
lending practices in this area.

These are just a few of the kinds of measures that should be considered. The basic thrust is that the current system of tax rules and financial regulation sets up a set of incentives and motivations that virtually
insure that the M&A and LBO craze will continue until it threatens
the financial condition of the entire corporate sector. At that point, the
debt-burdened companies will end up on the government's doorstep,
pleading for special assistance. And the government will be hard-pressed
to say no. That is not the kind of free enterprise system we ought to
have, one that speaks rhetorically of market disciplines but whispers in
the closet that the government will always bail people out if anything
really nasty happens. But it is the kind of system we will end up with if
nothing is done to introduce a more prudent regard for corporate capital than has been the case lately.

# 7

# *Shortcomings in Financial Oversight*

*Financial markets are ever-changing, and new technologies such as the Internet have only accelerated the pace of change. For this reason, the nation's chief official financial oversight body—the Federal Reserve—must be especially perceptive and responsive to structural changes in financial markets. When I gave this speech at the Federal Reserve Bank of Atlanta, Georgia, in March 1986, the deregulation of financial markets was relatively young. But that structural change and others I spoke about have proven to have profound effects.*

Today, more than ever, the financial system and its institutions are being transformed. It is important, therefore, to question how well the Federal Reserve, which was established many years ago, is structured, and whether it is adequately empowered to make a contribution to future economic and financial stability. We should ask what challenges face the Federal Reserve in implementing policies. How effective are its policies in a rapidly changing financial world? Should the role of the Fed be circumscribed and limited, or should the monetary and prudential responsibilities of this official institution be strengthened?

The Federal Reserve System was established in 1913 to cure four major defects in the U.S. financial system, and virtually all the significant developments that shaped its structure, operations, and effectiveness occurred prior to World War II. The major economic frailties at that time were:

1. There were problems associated with a highly decentralized commercial banking system; there was no national conservator of the money market. Instead, bank reserves were scattered and immobile. It was impossible to price these reserves in a national market.
2. Bank credit was unresponsive to seasonal and other needs.
3. The foreign exchange and money transfer system was inefficient.
4. The depository system for the U.S. Treasury contributed to the poor distribution of bank reserves and to banks' dependence on U.S. Treasury funds.

The next major pieces of legislation that affected the Federal Reserve were the Banking Acts of 1933 and 1935. This legislation established the Federal Deposit Insurance Corporation, prohibited interest on demand deposits, separated securities affiliates from commercial banks, created a Federal Open Market Committee, dissolved the old Federal Reserve Board and called for a Board of Governors, granted power to the Board of Governors to set differential reserve requirements according to "country" and "reserve city" bank classifications, and gave the Board the authority to regulate the rate of interest paid by member banks on time deposits.

Following World War II, the authority of the Federal Reserve System has been essentially unaltered except for the Treasury Accord of March 1951. The accord freed the Fed from its war-related obligations to support government bond prices, thus permitting the use of open market operations for economic stabilization purposes. The Fed later gained the authority to regulate bank holding companies. With only two exceptions, the Fed did not exercise its power pertaining to selective credit controls. First was the brief imposition of restraint on consumer and business credit in the spring of 1980. These controls were, for the most part, dismantled in 1981; margin requirements, however, remained in effect. Second was the recent imposition of margin requirements on selected kinds of high-yield, low-rated bond financing used for mergers and acquisitions that the Fed judged to be disguised equity.

While the authority and structure of the Fed have remained basically unchanged for many years, the U.S. financial markets differ radically from several decades ago and have certainly changed completely since 1913—when most of the country's financial structure was under the purview of the central bank. When the Federal Reserve was founded, total debt outstanding amounted to only $62 billion, compared with $7.7 trillion today. In 1912, there was only $1.3 billion of U.S. government debt and $15 billion of consumer and mortgage debt; business debt accounted for $36 billion, or 58 percent of the total outstanding. At present, U.S. government and federal credit agency debt amounts to $2.1 trillion, or 27 percent of total debt; consumer and mortgage debt totals $2.9 trillion, or 38 percent of total debt; and business debt now totals an estimated $2.1 trillion, or 27 percent of total debt.

In 1912, commercial banks were the dominant financial institution, holding $21 billion, or 65 percent, of the assets of all financial intermediaries. Although banks now have total assets of about $2 trillion, their relative importance in the financial system has diminished. A multiplicity of intermediaries—many of which did not exist in the United States in modern-day form in 1912—have come into great prominence, representing combined total assets of about $5.2 trillion, up from only $11 billion in 1912.

In addition to the much larger size of the U.S. credit market today, the Fed's task is further complicated by financial market developments that are beyond its direct jurisdiction. Specifically, five interrelated developments have important implications for the Federal Reserve: financial deregulation, financial innovation here and abroad, the growing securitization of financial markets, the globalization of financial markets, and the advancement of communications and technology.

Financial deregulation, in its many forms, has just about eliminated the barriers to competition among financial institutions. Captive savings in local and regional banking markets have virtually disappeared with the removal of interest rate ceilings on deposits. The broader lending and investing powers that have been granted to institutional participants have helped to blur the once well-defined demarcations among financial institutions. Everyone is trying to be in everyone else's business. The commercial banks want to be more like investment banks. The investment banks' balance sheets have commercial banking attributes. Thrift institutions want to be diversified lenders and investors. Nonbank lenders today enjoy some of the opportunities of banks. Contractual savings institutions are shortening the maturities of both assets and liabilities in order to compete more effectively with other institutions.

Regardless of the overall merits of deregulation, it was far easier in the past to conduct monetary policy effectively than it is today, because the formal structure that prevailed years ago—the compartmentalization of markets and institutions—made monetary restraint effective quite quickly. Years ago, the financial intermediaries were constrained; today, the risk of monetary restraint is passed on to the final demanders of credit. In the new financial world, more entities become substantial debtors even in periods of restraint, because under the spread banking approach—the quick raising of rates of return on assets as the cost of liabilities to financial intermediaries rises—final demanders of credit boost the price of credit, and the innovative suppliers are able to satisfy them until interest costs and associated risks become too high for borrowers. Monetary policy is thus rendered much more complex as we move into a more deregulated environment.

The competition induced by deregulation lowers the profit margins of financial institutions—in sharp contrast to the old comfortable spreads. For example, profit margins in housing finance have been reduced irregularly and gradually, and a similar, more radical squeeze will face institutions engaged in consumer credit. The response of financial institutions to this development, however, presents a serious challenge to the Fed. To maintain profitability, financial institutions have increased leverage and liberalized credit terms. In addition, not all institutions are well positioned to accept the competitive battle. Some are at a disadvantage because of the assets and liabilities they took on when markets were more structured. Other institutions do not quickly acquire the analytical and market talent to be viable in the new financial world. As a result, the Federal Reserve and other regulators are burdened with many weak financial institutions—some of which still function only because of artificial regulatory accounting practices and official financial support.

Another important development—financial innovation—often has benefited market participants. There is, however, no doubt that such changes have complicated the Federal Reserve's task. The Fed, as a limited participant in the U.S. government bond and foreign exchange markets, does not initiate financial innovation and, for the most part, is just an observer of the market process. As a result, the Fed learns about new instruments and financing techniques with a delay, and it therefore cannot quickly ascertain the implications of financial innovations for market developments or, more important, for monetary policy itself. The central bank is forced to play catch-up, while the market continuously circumvents monetary restraint through other financial innovations.

Consider, for example, the extent to which the Federal Reserve was able to incorporate in its policy actions the impact of the numerous financial innovations that were introduced or that became widely used during 1985. There were at least 35 such products, including, domestically, variable-duration notes, options on municipals, and commercial mortgage securities and, internationally, nondollar floating-rate notes, shogun bonds (U.S. dollar bonds issued in Japan), and European Currency Unit warrants.

To be sure, not all these innovations or variations on traditional instruments, nor all deregulatory actions, directly affect Fed policy, but many of the changes in recent years did leave their imprint on the measures that are targeted and monitored by the Federal Reserve. The velocity of the key monetary aggregates—especially M1—slowed drastically in 1985. M1 velocity, which used to increase annually by about 3¼ percent during the 1960s and 1970s, actually fell by 5½ percent in 1985. Part of the explanation for this decline is the fall in interest rates, and part also reflects a vain effort to change the definition of money in order to capture changes in money usage, which did not exist in an earlier period. Previously simple concepts have become complex: Ml has four money components; M2 has 10; and M3 has 14.

Another aspect of financial innovation, securitization, also has important ramifications for the central bank. Narrowly speaking, the securitization of credit is the changing of nonmarketable credit instruments into marketable form; in other words, it is the transformation of a nonmarketable instrument negotiated between borrower and lender into a tradable security. In a broader sense, it is any substitution of the open markets for the loan markets. This phenomenon is increasing in popularity in the United States and elsewhere. The ballooning of the U.S. government and federal credit agency debt is one important factor behind the growth of securitized obligations. The deposit market has also experienced securitization through brokered deposits, the issuance of negotiable CDs, and the need by institutions to quote market rates for deposits. Commercial paper issuance and the medium-term note market have mushroomed. High-yield, low-rated bonds have gained prominence. Floating-rate note financing has become popular worldwide. In addition, many proxy credit markets, including futures, options, interest rate swaps, and currency swaps, occasionally overshadow their spot market counterparts.

Consider the following open market developments in this new financial setting.

- The volume of outstanding domestic commercial paper now totals $299 billion, compared with $161 billion just five years ago.
- The average daily trading volume of U.S. note and bond futures amounted to $22 billion in January 1986, up from $8 billion in all of 1983.
- The average daily volume of trading in futures on money market instruments, including U.S. Treasury bills, certificates of deposit, and Eurodollar deposits amounted to $50 billion in January 1986, nearly 2.2 times the average daily volume in 1983.
- The turnover in outstanding U.S. bonds with a maturity of 10 years and longer was close to 15 times in 1985, in contrast to 3.8 times 10 years ago. Similarly, the turnover of U.S. Treasury notes with a maturity of five to 10 years rose to 14 times in 1985, up from 8.5 times in 1976.
- The volume of outstanding interest rate swaps—a market that hardly existed five years ago—has been estimated at about $150 billion.
- E. Gerald Corrigan, president of the Federal Reserve Bank of New York, recently stated that "it is not uncommon for the value of large dollar computerized payments processed by the New York Federal Reserve Bank and by the New York Clearing House to exceed $1 trillion in a single day."
- At Salomon Brothers, there have been days on which more than $75 billion has moved through our cashiering department, which is responsible for settling all of our transactions. This amount comprises the following: securities received and paid for by Salomon Brothers; securities delivered against funds received by Salomon Brothers; securities borrowed and securities lent; and, most significantly, the financing of our inventories.

These illustrations underscore the extent to which markets have developed beyond the direct jurisdiction of the Federal Reserve. Through securitization, as well as through deregulation, markets and financial institutions have become fungible. Changes in market price, whether reflected on balance sheets directly or de facto, impinge in turn on liquidity and capital requirements.

An even more important consequence is that securitization enhances the volume of open market transactions and the turnover of securities, which brings about at least two potential risks for the Federal Reserve. First, the accelerating pace of financial asset turnover may result in substantial "daylight" credit exposure, in the heavy use of leverage to garner quick profits, and in the overload of clearing arrangements involving participants that are beyond the immediate jurisdiction and responsibility of the central bank. Second, through securitization, financial intermediaries may sell off their highest-quality assets and acquire new assets of equal or perhaps weaker credit ratings. In a securitized world, banking spreads are market-determined rather than set through regulation. At times, this results in efforts to make these spreads regardless of credit quality.

Securitization also tends to create the illusion that credit risk can be reduced by the marketability of the credit instruments. The risk is that the disciplining force involved in the relationship between creditor and debtor is loosened, because creditors are not permanent holders of debt. Consequently, the credit problem has to be dealt with by either the open market or the monetary authorities. In a securitized world, the Fed will inherit the problem of the troublesome debtor, though today it has only limited control over the institutional arrangement that is fostering the problem.

Another phenomenon—the globalization of financial markets—presents different challenges to the Federal Reserve. Think of the rapidly increasing mobility and fluidity of today's global financial markets. The U.S. dollar markets extend far beyond our shores. U.S. and foreign institutions bid for their own and other currencies. Investment bankers underwrite issues denominated in several key currencies—and even multicurrency obligations are becoming more common. Increasingly, large borrowers are taking down funds in markets where they receive the best terms, be it New York, Tokyo, London, or Zurich. Many of the interest rate swap arrangements involve parties from different countries.

This globalization of financial markets naturally affects monetary policy. A traditional concern is that increased capital mobility makes it more difficult for central banks to control the domestic money supply. This is presumably less of an issue when exchange rates are freely floating but could again be an issue if we return to some form of managed exchange rates.

Globalization also has implications for bank regulatory and supervisory authorities, since many new credit instruments permit market participants in one country to arbitrage or to take advantage of opportunities in other nations. Some debt markets—Treasury securities, for example—now trade 24 hours a day, successively, around the world. While this does not nullify a country's monetary policy, in periods of monetary restraint the availability of funds outside a country allows some borrowers access to funds, thus requiring the central bank to reduce even further the internal availability of funds. Indeed, the growing importance of trade, capital flows, and exchange rates is impinging on domestic monetary policy decisions.

Exchange rate volatility has also been enhanced by the globalization of markets because of the availability of many liquid and marketable instruments, through which participants can quickly express their preferences. These opportunities were limited when much of the international market was confined to deposits or access was restricted by regulation.

Of course, the new financial setting could not flourish without the great advancements in communications and technology. Traders, portfolio managers, and financial officers of corporations have screens that transmit detailed economic and financial information almost instantaneously. Here is an incomplete list of the information and types of screens used by the traders at Salomon Brothers. Traders view screens that transmit foreign exchange quotations and developments; broker quotes on all major debt markets; transactions on all major exchanges (securities, commodities, and international exchanges such as Liffe); graphic displays, such as trends in futures and options; and electronic market-making activity such as Instinet and NASDAQ. In addition, with video screens, traders can retrieve trade data, research reports, price histories on securities, and account information.

Aside from video display terminals, there is an extensive telecommunications capability. Our main office has about 6,000 dial telephone lines and roughly 2,000 direct-access lines. Traders have access to up to 120 multiple dialing and direct lines. The typical news services—including Dow Jones News Wire, Dow Jones Capital Markets Report, Reuters, Knight Ridder, and MuniFacts—are scattered throughout the firm, and other influential wire services include the Associated Press and United Press International.

In addition, new economic and financial information is interpreted and delivered to users with great speed. The result is lightning-fast responsiveness by traders and portfolio managers. Thus, we can have outsized price movements from larger-than-expected swings in the weekly money supply data or in monthly economic indicators. In addition, through its effect on markets, the rapid dissemination of information around the world creates a disciplining force on policy makers.

Financial markets have been changed radically by these five developments, and it is therefore essential to reexamine the role of central banking.

The question then becomes: How should this new financial world be managed, or should it be managed at all? Some urge that the discipline of the marketplace should prevail—let institutions fail if they incur undue risk and are reckless. I believe this advocacy is naive and unrealistic.

While we, as Americans, generally favor letting the market determine winners and losers, there are limits to this approach with regard to financial institutions. Financial institutions, unlike business corporations, have huge liabilities with proportionately smaller capital bases, and even more important, they have liabilities that represent temporary funds and savings of the public. Such entities also do not stand alone; their assets and liabilities are intertwined with those of many other financial institutions both here and abroad.

One of the unusual aspects of the current situation is that as the financial markets become increasingly competitive, and aggressive financial practices are evident in markets and at financial institutions, the public safety net is spreading through official actions and through market developments. The decision to prevent a default of the Continental Illinois Bank and to protect the creditors of its holding company is evidence that market forces will not be allowed to exercise the full discipline over large institutions. Moreover, the depositors of smaller institutions have enjoyed the protection of the safety net. To remove deposit insurance today from banks would be an unthinkable form of market discipline. Federal support for farm credit agencies covers, in part, another sector. Obligations covered by private credit insurance, including some commercial paper, mortgages, municipal obligations, and the implied guarantee by the federal government of many other federal credit obligations also spread the official safety net, because again, large private institutions and federal credit agencies will probably not be permitted to default.

In essence, we have a rapidly growing credit structure, aggressive risk taking, and decreasing direct control by the central bank over many aspects of the marketplace—but all in the context of a broadening official safety net. This is a dangerous combination. Where are the disciplines in the system? There is a false sense of security about this matter today, because we are in a period of substantial monetary accommodation. Market pressures have eased, but new abuses are occurring whose effects will surface later on, when the central bank has to step back from its current policy.

One implication of all these developments for monetary policy is that there are no simple rules for conducting policy. Changes brought about through deregulation, innovation, and securitization render obsolete the meaning of money supply and its strict use as a policy tool. Nonetheless, there is no realistic possibility of substituting some other simplistic concept as policy variables: It will also be found obsolete eventually as market participants adapt their behavior and strive to overcome policy restraints through new instruments and financing techniques here and abroad. The Fed will always find itself in a position of having to build a better mousetrap.

Many years ago, I suggested that, given the emerging changes in the financial system, the Federal Reserve set targets for the growth of debt. The Fed did adopt a credit monitor a few years ago, but I suspect that this, too, is now an ineffective tool. There is too much debt being created that is not officially recorded or known. Off-balance-sheet debt exceeds balance-sheet debt in some instances. The netting of assets and liabilities is widespread. If the credit aggregate is to be effective, the collection of credit data will have to be improved vastly.

The new financial world encumbers the Fed with a poorly defined monetary approach. The central bank is forced to be highly judgmental, as changing variables come to the fore in the implementation of policy. This, in itself, requires that the Fed have insight into rapidly changing financial developments and their policy implications. Even if it has these insights and they are timely, they still may not necessarily serve as a basis for an effective policy. With so much of these changes beyond the direct control of the Federal Reserve, the monetary guidance mechanism is bound to be faulty.

In formulating remedies to this problem, we must recognize that markets and institutions are no longer compartmentalized, that money is a blurred and changing concept, and that the new features of our financial world require different rules, regulations, and official governing arrangements. In this altered setting, does it make sense to have so many regulators? Do we need the Federal Reserve, the Federal Home

Loan Banks, the Federal Deposit Insurance Corporation, the Federal Savings and Loan Insurance Corporation, the Comptroller of the Currency, the Securities and Exchange Commission, and state supervisory authorities?

The need is for centralized monitoring and regulation of our credit system. In this connection, there are at least two solutions: (1) The prudential responsibilities of the Federal Reserve could be enlarged to include institutions other than banks; or (2) as I suggested in congressional testimony in 1985, a National Board of Overseers of Financial Institutions should be established. Such a board should promulgate uniform accounting standards, improve reporting procedures, work toward fuller disclosure of information, and provide an integrated view and periodic policy directives concerning institutions, market practices, and trading activity. Members of the Board of Governors of the Federal Reserve should be part of such a Board of Overseers, and it should also include knowledgeable personnel from other institutional groups.

The regulations that need to be imposed on our credit system cannot be a return to the structure that existed several decades ago. Too much has changed in the composition of the markets. If failure is an unacceptable form of discipline, then institutions and markets should adhere to standards that prevent them from moving to the precipice of failure. The Federal Reserve is moving in the right direction—witness its call for higher capital ratios on a more broadly defined capital base and its ruling on high-yield, low-rated bonds, which I believe was a symbolic gesture showing concern. At best, this is only a beginning.

If financial institutions are going to be involved in the open credit market, in trading, in underwriting, and in swapping assets of all sorts, then they should also be required to state their assets at the lower of cost or market. Losses would be recognized quickly, thus putting pressure on managements to pursue reasonable practices. Failure to use this principle in the case of the debt crisis in developing countries has complicated the search for a solution dramatically because of the need to maintain the par value of outstanding loans. Had this principle been utilized, the value of these loans would have been reduced prior to the onset of the crisis. While some may claim that not all assets can be readily priced at market, this alleged handicap is overstated today. More obligations are now marketable, and official supervisors should be relied upon to provide realistic valuations for the rest. Opposition to this more conservative approach is shortsighted, because it is based on the immediate negative earnings impact and fails to recognize the ongoing benefit to the strength of financial institutions and to the integrity of the entire credit system.

Some have advocated a market approach to deposit insurance by having risk-related premiums. At first blush, this type of premium seems appealing, but it also has some drawbacks. For example, noninsured creditors of deposit institutions would surely consider withdrawing their credit from an institution that pays a high premium rate. This, in turn, may force the institution to pay higher rates on insured deposits and to try to offset this cost by making riskier loans and investments. I would prefer that all institutions be rated by their official supervisory agencies and that the ratings be released to the public with a one-year delay. This would allow an institution to take steps to remedy its problems and would enable the supervisory agency to issue an addendum to the rating. The supervisory agencies have a much more intimate knowledge of the financial institutions under their purview than do private rating agencies, and by their nature, they have a greater capacity to enforce change.

In the wake of the financial revolution, some strides are being made by the central banks of the major industrial nations to cope with the impact of international market linkages. Despite the improved monitoring of developments, the authorities have a long way to go before they can deal effectively with currency swaps, multicurrency bonds, market clearing risks, the huge volume of currency transactions, and international arbitraging and hedging activities.

Here, too, a formalized official institution needs to be organized. It should consist of central bankers and other officials that will set standards and monitor developments in the international credit markets, and it needs to be given power and authority. In time, capital requirements, accounting standards, and financial reports of multinational institutions will have to be more uniform if direct official intervention in the market is to be avoided. Indeed, if markets are to continue to move more and more toward open, rather than negotiated, transactions, and if the linkage between debtor and creditor is to be interrupted by frequent shifts of the creditor, then we must have increased financial disclosure by all participants, domestic and international; and that includes commercial and investment banks and contractual and discretionary savings institutions. More debt will have to be brought "onto" balance sheets, and less netting of assets and liabilities will be essential in a world that is prone to leveraging and that is increasingly willing to take risks.

I also believe that new efforts to stabilize exchange rates cannot succeed without credit market coordination among central banks in the industrial world. To be sure, underlying economic differences will always leave their mark on currency values—as they should. Limiting excessive currency volatility, however, in mobile international marketplaces cannot be accomplished without considering the differences in capital requirements, accounting standards, and market practices that prevail among countries.

Given the enlarged reach of institutions and markets and the Fed's limited direct authority over many financial activities, the risk is greater that the Federal Reserve will be politicized and that its autonomy will be diminished. This will occur because the task will be beyond the capacity of the Fed—and of other regulators—to spread a broadening safety net and still enforce discipline. This risk will hit home the next time significant monetary restraint needs to be imposed. Politicizing monetary policy is dangerous, for, among other reasons, a political monetary policy will focus on accomplishing very near-term objectives, rather than achieving a longer-term steadying influence. A politicized Fed will also make it difficult, at times, to impose the restraint that conditions dictate; the political leadership may not be willing to accept the criticism from vested interest groups. I do not, therefore, share the view that the term of the chairman of the Federal Reserve Board of Governors should be coterminous with that of the president of the United States. There should not be a Republican or Democratic monetary policy. There is only one correct monetary policy.

The effectiveness of the Federal Reserve will also be harmed if the salary of governors, who are asked to serve for 14 years, remains at $73,600 annually and only $75,000 for the chairman. Is this adequate, given their overwhelming responsibility—guardian of the commercial banks, which have assets of $2 trillion, and indirect overseers of the $7.7 trillion total debt structure of the United States? For this task, more generous compensation is clearly in order. These people have to be attracted from the best that is available in the academic, business, and financial world. The politicizing of the Federal Reserve might also be eased somewhat if the discount rate became a flexible rate hinged directly to movements in money market rates based on a known formula. While the Federal Reserve and others have occasionally favored such a direct linkage, it has not yet been adopted.

In conclusion, it is time to recognize the implications for monetary policy of our new financial world. The Federal Reserve has decreasing direct control over a financial system that is bulging in size and complexity and that has mobile instruments and fungible assets that enable funds to be shifted rapidly through the country and across borders. The Federal Reserve needs to be strengthened—and its powers broadened—if the financial markets are to serve the economy well and the economy is not to become the servant of the market.

# PART III
# THE BIGNESS DILEMMA

# 8

# From Financial Segmentation to Concentration

In a single generation, our financial system has been transformed. After operating for centuries as a constellation of specialized services, it has melded together rapidly into a highly concentrated oligopoly of enormous, diversified, integrated firms. This revolution has gone largely unnoticed.

Many of these institutions have operated independently for decades or, in a few cases, centuries. Commercial banks served as safe harbors for savings and sources of business and household capital. Insurance companies curbed catastrophic risk by sharing it among policy holders. Stock and bond houses underwrote new and expanding enterprises. Mortgage companies and thrifts enabled widespread home ownership. Pension funds managed corporate retirement funds. More recently, mutual fund companies and credit card firms have gathered middle-class capital, while branchless (online) banks brought financial services into the home.

To be sure, financial concentration is hardly new. In the Middle Ages, European monarchs granted charters to financial institutions, which played central roles in financing wars and other kingly enterprises.

During the Age of Exploration, the British crown granted monopoly charters to joint-stock companies such as the East India Company, which operated in South Asia, and the Virginia Company (1606) and the Massachusetts Bay Company (1629), which colonized British North America. After the Revolutionary War put an end to British mercantilism in the new United States, the First and Second Banks of the United States were quasi-public institutions designed to strengthen and stabilize the money supply. The Gilded Age of the late nineteenth century, dominated by J. Pierpont Morgan, ushered in new concerns about a so-called money trust, yet investment banks served the needs of the burgeoning economy extremely well.

But early financial concentration gradually gave way to specialization, as both a cause and an effect of economic development. As societies grow and as the volume of their commercial transactions multiplies, specialists are needed. Historically, the change has come at different times in different nations, but the American case is illustrative. In colonial times, diversified general merchants served simultaneously as lenders, insurers, investors, shippers, and traders. After the American Revolution, all-purpose sedentary merchants were eclipsed by the first specialized banks, stock exchanges, wholesalers, factors, and insurance companies. The Bank of North America was founded in 1781, the Bank of the United States in 1791, the Insurance Company of North America in 1792, and the Philadelphia Stock Exchange—the nation's first—in 1800. Throughout the nineteenth century, specialized firms multiplied to serve the needs of an increasingly urban, industrialized nation.

In the twentieth century, two events transformed money and banking and led to even greater specialization. First, the Great Depression of the 1930s inspired a sweeping political backlash against the speculative excesses of the 1920s. Congress passed a wave of tough legislation that constrained financial institutions, chiefly banks, within specified markets and segregated them from many activities. The new laws imposed ceilings on interest rates that deposit institutions could pay on time deposits and savings deposits—even on interest that banks would charge on residential mortgages. These laws further segmented the activities of financial institutions: Financial conglomerates not only became unfashionable, they were outlawed as well.

Second, World War II solidified and strengthened the system. U.S. financial institutions entered the postwar years in a highly liquid position holding a large volume of U.S. government securities and very little in private debt. After playing a key role in war finance, they held high-quality investments and boasted sound capital ratios. For many of their managers, the harrowing banking failures and massive debt write-offs of the Depression years were fresh memories. It was reasonable to expect that financial specialization—with its segmented and well-defined silos—would endure indefinitely. In most cases, the name of a firm clearly signaled its business, with words such as "Savings and Loan" or "Mutual" or "Investment" or "Commercial."

The consolidation of American financial institutions gradually increased in the 1960s and 1970s and became even more perceptible in the 1980s. It gathered momentum in the 1990s and rose dramatically as the current credit crisis took hold. In the early period, it centered mainly on the mergers of banking institutions, especially of deposit-type institutions such as commercial banks and savings and loan associations. Many institutions that lost their independence were the victims of excessive banking practices that came to the fore during credit crises. Later on, in the 1990s and early in this decade, voluntary acquisitions were actively sought in the marketplace. No matter how one views the trend in financial concentration in the United States, the trend has been extremely dramatic. This is demonstrated in Exhibit 8.1, which shows the share of U.S. financial assets held by the 10, 20, and 50 largest financial institutions. The 10 largest, which as late as 1990 held only 10 percent, now hold more than 50 percent. The 20 largest institutions now hold more than 70 percent, as compared with 12 percent at the start of the 1990s. Indeed, prior to about the 1990s, there had been a downward tilt in the concentration percentages.

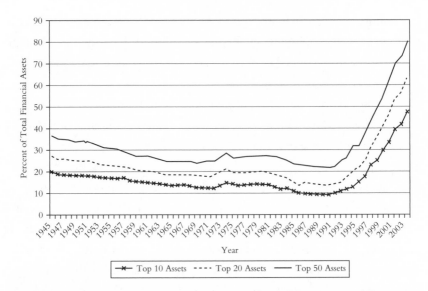

**Exhibit 8.1**   Top Financial Companies' Share of Total U.S. Financial Assets, 1945–2004

Sources: *The Banker*, 1993–2004; *Fortune*, 2005; Federal Reserve Flow of Funds, 1993–2003, L109.

Each major individual institutional grouping became part of this consolidation movement into financial conglomerates—or, as some call them, integrated financial institutions. For most of the twentieth century, U.S. deposit institutions were confined in a two-tiered structure. At the top were a small number of very large firms. Below the giants were many small and medium-size institutions. That was particularly so in the decades that immediately followed World War II. Then came a dramatic reversal. Small and medium-size deposit institutions began to disappear—some through outright failure, while many others were gobbled up by larger banks.

The disappearance of the thrift institutions already was noted, but it has been especially pronounced in commercial banks. At the end of 1985, there were more than 18,000 Federal Deposit Insurance Corporation (FDIC) member banks (see Exhibit 8.2). By the end of 2007, the number had fallen to 8,534. In 1985, the 10 largest U.S. commercial

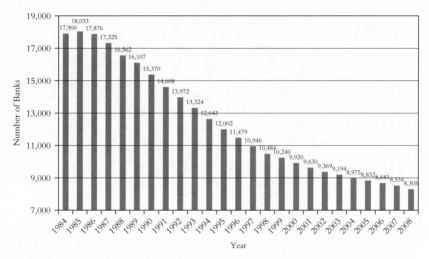

**Exhibit 8.2**　Number of Banks Insured by the Federal Deposit Insurance Corporation (Year-End)

banks accounted for 15 percent of all commercial bank assets. Between 1985 and 2008, the share of total bank assets held by the top four U.S. commercial banks more than doubled, from 12 percent to 30 percent.

While these statistics on banking concentration are by themselves startling, the effect is reinforced by a look at which institutions survived and which disappeared since 1991. Of the 15 largest banks that year, all but five have lost their independence. As shown in Exhibit 8.3, nine of these institutions were acquired or merged into the five remaining institutions. Only Citigroup, Bank of America, JPMorgan Chase, Wells Fargo, and PNC Financial have survived, while one other was acquired by a Geneva bank. Moreover, in 1991, these 15 large institutions had total assets of $1.2 trillion. The surviving five had total footings of $6.3 trillion in mid-2008.

In the mutual fund industry, concentration remains high. At the end of 2007, the top five managers controlled 38 percent of the industry's assets. This concentration ratio was 50 percent for the top 10, and 71 percent for the top 25 investment companies.

**Exhibit 8.3**   Largest U.S. Banks, 1991 and 2008

Largest U.S. Banks, June 30, 1991

| Bank Holding Company | Total Assets (billions of dollars) |
|---|---|
| Citicorp | $ 217 |
| BankAmerica Corp. | 113 |
| Chase Manhattan | 99 |
| J.P. Morgan | 97 |
| Security Pacific | 80 |
| Chemical Banking Corp. | 74 |
| NCNB | 69 |
| Manufacturers Hanover | 61 |
| Bankers Trust | 59 |
| Wells Fargo | 54 |
| First Interstate | 50 |
| First Chicago | 48 |
| Fleet/Norstar | 48 |
| PNC Financial | 44 |
| First Union | 40 |
| Total | $1,153 |

Survivors, December 31, 2008

| Bank Holding Company | Total Assets (billions of dollars) |
|---|---|
| Citigroup | $1,938 |
| Bank of America | 1,817 |
| JPMorgan Chase | 2,175 |
| Wells Fargo | 1,309 |
| PNC Financial | 291 |
| Total | $8,913 |

SOURCES: Company Reports, EDGAR, Bloomberg.

Independent Wall Street investment banking firms probably were uprooted most profoundly by mergers or bankruptcies. Some of the early casualties included such prominent firms as E.F. Hutton, Kidder Peabody, PaineWebber, and Dean Witter Reynolds. In 1988, the leading firms in the offerings of corporate debt, mortgage-backed securities, municipal obligations, and equities included Goldman Sachs, Merrill Lynch, Salomon Brothers, First Boston, Morgan Stanley, Shearson Lehman Brothers, Drexel Burnham Lambert, Prudential-Bache, and Bear Stearns. Of these nine firms, only two remained independent at the end of 2008: Goldman Sachs and Morgan Stanley. Bear Stearns had been acquired by JPMorgan Chase, Lehman had failed, and Merrill Lynch was bought by the Bank of America. Goldman Sachs and Morgan Stanley rushed under the Federal Reserve umbrella by putting their organizations into a bank holding company structure. Virtually all the investment banking stalwarts—many of which carried the names of their founders and were household names—are now part of a corporate identity with multiple lineages and with monikers that embody little, if any, historical significance.

For their part, insurers, too, have bent to the winds of consolidation. After hovering around $600 million since the end of World War II, the average assets of U.S. life insurers began to shoot up in the middle 1980s, and topped $1.6 billion in 2000. Here, again, assets commanded by the top 10 to 25 firms became more concentrated. By early 2009, the largest U.S. insurance company, American International Group (AIG), had been taken over by the federal government.

Health insurance, an imposing business that is growing by leaps and bounds, also is becoming more and more concentrated. Since the late 1990s, more than 350 health insurers and managed-care organizations have combined to narrow the field considerably. The American Medical Association recently found that health insurers in the vast majority of both rural and urban areas are very concentrated in the combined health maintenance organization (HMO)/preferred provider organization (PPO) market, a trend they see as unhealthy. According to regulators, concentration levels are high in three-quarters of all U.S. markets. And at the highest level, the top 10 firms insure an astonishing half of all insured Americans.

Typically, those who attempt to evaluate the U.S. financial system rely on traditional measures as found on balance sheets, profit and loss statements, annual reports, and 10-K reports. In the past 30 years or so, however, such data have become largely outmoded. The reason, as noted earlier, is the fundamentally different nature of today's leading financial institutions. If a bank is no longer a bank, an insurance company is no longer an insurance company, and so on, then the measures developed to gauge the solvency, risk taking, and performance of such financial institutions no longer are fully relevant.

One can begin to get a fuller and more accurate picture by scrutinizing footnotes that discuss off-balance-sheet assets. But even that data cannot be aggregated to show the total involvement of the conglomerates in financial markets. We can begin to comprehend the enormity of the involvement of the large integrated financial institutions in our financial system by considering the relationship of their total assets to gross domestic product (GDP) or to total nonfinancial debt. Their involvement is far greater when viewed from their activities in key sectors of the financial markets. This is quite evident from the data in Exhibit 8.4. It shows the involvement in key activities of the surviving large financial institutions at year-end 2007. Added to this data of the individual institutions are also the data of the institutions that were independent in 2007 but were merged into the institutions shown in the table. For these remaining institutions, the total involvement in the financial markets—consisting of their stated assets, off-balance-sheet guarantees or commitments, gross notional derivatives underwritten, and assets under management for others—totaled $244 trillion. To be sure, these are not all liabilities, but rather one rough measure of financial market involvement that is far from complete. Nevertheless, these 15 financially integrated institutions show total net equity of only $78 billion. This is a remarkable reach into financial market activity, especially considering the relatively small total equity of the institutions involved.

In March 2007, the Federal Reserve Bank of New York published data that revealed startling degrees of concentration in financial markets. From 1990 to 2004, 5 percent of institutions accounted for 61 percent of all underwriting of initial public offerings, 56 percent of investment-grade

**Exhibit 8.4** Total Assets, Shareholders Equity, and Key Activities of the 15 Largest U.S. Financial Institutions as of December 31, 2007 (Billions of Dollars)

| | Total Assets | Off-Balance–Sheet Commitments | Gross Notional Derivatives Underwritten | Assets Under Management/ Advisory | Total Activity | Shareholders' Equity |
|---|---|---|---|---|---|---|
| Citigroup | $ 2,187 | $1,244 | $ 82,756 | $1,784 | $ 87,971 | $114 |
| Bank of America | 1,715 | 1,487 | 32,669 | 640 | 36,511 | 147 |
| JPMorgan Chase | 1,562 | 1,265 | 77,249 | 1,600 | 81,676 | 123 |
| Morgan Stanley* | 1,045 | 110 | 7,120 | 782 | 9,057 | 31 |
| Merrill Lynch | 1,020 | 45 | 4,562 | 1,400 | 7,027 | 32 |
| Wells Fargo | 575 | 936 | 1,028 | 936 | 3,475 | 48 |
| AIG | 1,060 | 275 | 2,132 | 94 | 3,561 | 96 |
| Wachovia | 782 | 145 | 5,003 | 84 | 6,013 | 77 |
| MetLife | 558 | 5 | 210 | | 773 | 35 |
| Prudential | 485 | 14 | 78 | 648 | 1,224 | 23 |
| Hartford | 360 | 2 | 28 | 56 | 445 | 19 |
| Washington Mutual | 327 | | 2 | | 329 | 25 |
| Allstate | 156 | 3 | 53 | | 212 | 22 |
| Lehman* | 691 | 112 | 737 | 282 | 1,822 | 22 |
| Goldman Sachs* | 1,119 | 214 | 2,045 | 868 | 4,246 | 43 |
| Total | $13,642 | $5,856 | $215,672 | $9,173 | $244,344 | $857 |

*November 2007.

SOURCES: Company reports, EDGAR, company 10-Ks, Henry Kaufman & Company research.

bonds, and 56 percent of high-yield bonds. From 1995 to 2004, the top 5 percent of institutions, classified as primary dealers, accounted for 38 percent of the transactions in Treasury bills, 42 percent of coupon issues, 58 percent of mortgage bonds, and 74 percent of the transactions in corporate obligations.

"Our review of trends in financial market structure," noted the authors of the report, "yields two main findings. First, while high and rising concentration is not universal, some markets are indeed highly concentrated or increasingly so. Second, financial markets are becoming more interdependent, and the same set of large institutions is increasingly likely to occupy top ranking in several markets."

In looking over the span of years since World War II, several features stand out about financial concentration. First, as noted at the beginning of this chapter, we entered the postwar period with a highly segmented arrangement for financial institutions. Second, financial institutions were highly liquid at the time. Third, they were still overcoming the memory of the financial devastation caused by the Great Depression. Fourth, financial concentration increased only slowly, gaining momentum during the past two decades (the most pronounced increase occurred during the past decade). Fifth, the latest credit crisis increased concentration by leaps and bounds. Sixth, during this crisis official policy makers actually encouraged huge financial institutions to merge in order to avoid insolvency and market disruptions. Seventh, by its actions and encouragement, official policy acknowledged what a large number of experts understood—that many large institutions are deemed too big to fail. That realization is bound to cause changes in how we supervise and regulate financial institutions and in the conduct of monetary policy, the topic of a later chapter.

# 9

# Financial Concentration in Economic Thought

In many ways the field of economics began with its first great theorist, the Scottish genius Adam Smith, whose work of synthesis, *The Wealth of Nations*, appeared the same year as the American Declaration of Independence. Unlike his contemporaries—mercantilists, who looked to government to provide special monopoly protections, and physiocrats, who believed that agriculture was the only productive sector—Smith believed that industry, even finance, could create taxable surplus. To allow markets to work their wonders, Smith advocated in favor of free international trade and limited government interference in the economy, a position that has made his work a touchstone for the advocates of unhindered markets ever since.

A closer look at Smith's writings reveals interesting nuances on the question of banking and financial concentration. Smith supported the regulation of banks. Most notably, he insisted on the convertibility of banknotes and deposits into specie on demand, and urged the prohibition of banknotes of small denomination (which in his day meant less than £10 in London or less than £5 outside the metropolis). These regulations were intended to maintain adequate specie reserves, while redemption of liabilities for specie, Smith reasoned, would serve to test a bank's liquidity. Today's central banks pursue the same goals through different means. In Smith's day, banks that issued small notes without discipline usually failed.

Smith recognized the high costs of such failures. Bank failures, he wrote, created "a very great calamity, to many poor people who had received their notes in payment." As for the regulation of banks, the great champion of laissez-faire recognized the special character of banks as custodians of wealth, and the risks to society if they are left in irresponsible hands: "[T]hose exertions of the natural liberty of a few individuals, which might endanger the security of the whole society, are, and ought to be, restrained by the laws of all governments, of the most free as well as of the most despotical."

Smith was a stalwart guardian of personal liberty. Yet he believed regulations that safeguard the broader society from danger are just and proper. "The obligation of building party walls, in order to prevent the communication of fire," he elaborated, "is a violation of natural liberty, exactly of the same kind with the regulations of the banking trade which are here proposed." Governments should not allow financial institutions, or anyone else for that matter, to play with fire.

At the same time, Smith was no advocate of what became known as the "too big to fail" doctrine—or any other safety net for financial institutions. In his long description of the failure of the Ayr Bank, he never once hints that anyone apart from the bank's proprietors should pay the bank's debts—this despite the fact that some of his "friends," including his sponsor, the Duke of Baccleuch, were "deeply concerned" (that is, invested) in the ill-fated enterprise. Smith even helped some of his friends, who were fully liable for the failed bank's debts, to liquidate some of their assets in order to meet the calls of the bank's creditors.

Smith was no big fan of the Bank of England, the semiprivate, semipublic quasi-central institution that dominated British banking in the eighteenth century. At one point he sarcastically refers to it as "this great company" because it had been on "occasions . . . reduced to the necessity of paying sixpences." Smith feared that the financial system relied too much on the Bank of England. Should an enemy seize London, and hence the specie supporting the credit of the Bank of England's notes, "confusion" would reign. Barter or credit would be the only mechanisms for making exchanges. In this way, Smith highlighted the risks of concentrating too many financial eggs in one basket.

That Smith abhorred monopoly in banking should not surprise us, for he took pains to argue that "in general, if any branch of trade, or any division of labor, be advantageous to the public, the freer and more general the competition," the better. He also castigated businessmen for conspiring—with each other and with governments—to reduce competition. "People of the same trade seldom meet together," he chided, "even for merriment and diversion, but the conversation ends in conspiracy against the public, or in some contrivance to raise prices."

Smith clearly influenced Alexander Hamilton, America's famous first Treasury secretary. Hamilton felt that with a good central bank in place, the more state banks, the better. He helped establish two state banks: the Bank of New York and Merchants' Bank. He may have even quietly supported the creation of the Manhattan Company, a project led by Aaron Burr, a rival who would kill him in a duel. Though Hamilton played with the idea of merging the state banks with the central bank, the Bank of the United States, he thought better of it. He believed that a central bank could ensure that state banks held adequate reserves by promptly returning their liabilities to them in exchange for specie. In this way, like Smith, Hamilton saw the need to moderate risk taking of banks in order to stabilize the financial system.

David Ricardo, the first of the great nineteenth-century classical economists, differed from Smith and Hamilton on many fine points of economic theory, even monetary theory, but not on the major precepts of the proper regulation of money and banking. A wealthy financier and landowner, Ricardo nevertheless was sympathetic to the plight of the poor, though he did not go so far as to favor wealth redistribution. Little wonder, then, that his major work, *The Principles of Political Economy and Taxation*, did not explicitly discuss financial concentration. But he was

even more critical of the Bank of England than Smith had been, asserting in 1809 that "all the evils of our currency were owing to the over-
issues of the Bank, to the dangerous power with which it was entrusted
of diminishing at its will, the value of every man's property." Ricardo
also blamed the Bank of England for the 1797 panic that led it to sus-
pend the convertibility of its liabilities. "If the Bank had continued paying cash, probably the panic would have subsided before their coin had
been exhausted." The Bank's directors, in other words, had placed their
self-interest above that of the national economy—a risk inherent in any
capitalist system in which a small number of investors holds inordinate
sway over the larger society's financial well-being.

John Stuart Mill was another classical economist who advocated the
regulation of financial institutions. Mill clearly believed that those who
overtraded and got caught ought to suffer the consequences, and the
more quickly, the better for all. "It must be admitted," he argued, that
increased bank accommodation during speculative bubbles "enables the
speculative prices to be kept up for some time after they would otherwise have collapsed; and therefore prolongs and increases the drain of
the precious metals for exportation, which is a leading feature of this
stage in the progress of a commercial crisis." The drain of specie, he went
on to explain, made banks reduce their loans after the crash even more
drastically than they otherwise would need to do.

Mill also had some very harsh words for bankers, at least those "south
of the Tweed" (south of Scotland). "The almost incredible instances of
reckless and fraudulent mismanagement" on the part of England's corporate banks "have shown only too clearly that . . . the joint-stock principle
applied to banking is not the adequate safeguard it was so confidently
supposed to be." He concluded, then, that if banks were to be allowed
to issue notes, "some kind of special security in favour of the holders of
notes should be exacted as an imperative condition." He refrained from
giving details, but may have had in mind some sort of deposit insurance
or extra stockholder liability.

It may seem more than a little ironic that Mill, who is probably most famous for his stirring defense of human freedom in his short 1859 book, *On Liberty*, advocated banking regulation. The key to unlocking the apparent contradiction is Mill's definition of freedom. "The only freedom which deserves the name," he wrote, "is that of pursuing our own good in our own way, *so long as we do not attempt to deprive others of theirs, or impede their efforts to obtain it.*" (emphasis added) In other words, society has the right to restrict dangerous activities—like banking! In addition, Mill's desire to regulate financial institutions is not surprising given that he was a close follower of Adam Smith, who, as noted, held very similar views of banking and regulation.

As a classical economist and liberal (in the eighteenth-century meaning of the word), Mill clashed with Europe's rising socialist economists, including Karl Marx, the preeminent critic of capitalism and father of communism. Marx and Friedrich Engels saw nothing wrong with financial concentration, provided the state owned and operated the bank or banks. As early as his 1847 "The Principles of Communism," Engels called for the "centralization of money and credit in the hands of the state through a national bank with state capital, and the suppression of all private banks and bankers." In *The Communist Manifesto*, Marx and Engels set forth the same idea in slightly less ominous terms, calling for the "centralization of credit in the banks of the state, by means of a national bank with state capital and an exclusive monopoly." Later revolutionaries who followed in Marx's steps heeded those instructions carefully. Vladimir Lenin argued that "a single State Bank, the biggest of the big, with branches in every rural district, in every factory, will constitute as much as nine-tenths of commercial and savings bank branches."

The Marxists proved to be wrong about banking. They were also wrong about which countries would adopt their nostrums. Germany, Britain, the United States, and other industrialized nations did not fall. But there did arise in the West in the twentieth century a school of economic thought that advocated much more powerful government interdiction in the economy than had any classical economist. This school, named for its leading light, John Maynard Keynes, stemmed not from socialist thought but from a branch of the classical school that led from Mill to the late nineteenth- and early twentieth-century British economist Alfred Marshall.

Although heavily influenced by Mill and other classical economists, Marshall eventually broke from that tradition, much to the improvement of economic science. Mill was especially troubled by the boom-and-bust cycle that had so plagued the Western economies in the nineteenth century. On the one hand, Marshall advocated the expansion of the discretionary power of a bank's directors in accord with "their knowledge of the special circumstances of each case." But rather than extend help to troubled institutions after an asset bubble had burst, Marshall wanted to keep all institutions, financial and otherwise, sound by preventing periods of speculative fever in the first place. "I hold very strongly," he told the Gold and Silver Committee, "that by far the greatest evil that we have to deal with is the occasional pressure in the money market." Similarly, he told the members of the Indian Currency Committee in 1899, "a fall of prices [of bonds and other property] of this kind is seldom or never the product of natural causes."

Like Mill and other classical economists, Marshall understood that sometimes bankers went bad. "Some scarcely tried to make their way for sure," he complained, "for so long as they could appear to be rich, it mattered little to them whether they were wasting the property of their customers. They speculated boldly." But "the evils of reckless trading," Marshall saw quite clearly, "are always apt to spread far beyond the persons immediately concerned," which too often meant "people of small means." In words that soon proved prophetic, for the Great Depression was on the near horizon, the great classical economist warned that "the failure of one bank caused distrust to rage around others and to bring down banks that were really solid; as the fire spreads from one wooden house to another, till even nearly fire-proof buildings succumb in the blaze of a great conflagration."

The Great Depression produced a great economist. As noted, John Maynard Keynes came out of the Marshall school, yet he, too, broke important new ground. His work addressed the inescapable economic conundrum of the day, the harrowing and seemingly interminable economic depression that held most of the world in its grip in the 1930s. Keynes saw governments as key in breaking the economic stranglehold, first, through monetary action, and second, through massive deficit spending. The fiscal and monetary stimuli that Keynes advocated were systemic and large-scale, not bailouts of individual firms. In effect, Keynes was trying to induce governments to bail out entire economies. Running through Keynes's various proposals was a basic distrust of the unfettered workings of the market, especially the stock market. "When the capital development of a country becomes a by-product of the activities of a casino," he warned colorfully, "the job is likely to be ill done."

Keynes' theories and policies held sway in the United States for much of the post–World War II era, when economic policy makers actively and confidently intervened to fine-tune the economy for sustained growth. A succession of presidents, beginning with John F. Kennedy, saw deficit spending as an easy fix. But as stagflation gripped the nation in the 1970s, Keynesianism began to fall out of fashion, supplanted by the ideas of monetarists such as Milton Friedman and Austrian economists who similarly spurned regulation in favor of unfettered markets.

Friedman was born in Brooklyn in 1912 to poor Jewish immigrants. Rather than see his mother's job as a sweatshop seamstress as a sign of capitalism's dark side, he viewed it as a means to human emancipation. His family was poor, but the nation was meritocratic enough to allow its bright, hardworking citizens to excel. That is just what Friedman did, learning from the best minds in economics at the University of Chicago and Columbia University. Friedman's staunch advocacy of free markets and cutting-edge critique of most forms of government interdiction (popularized in his best-selling book *Free to Choose*) set the ideological stage for the regulatory liberalization movements of the 1970s, 1980s, and 1990s—including deregulation of financial services.

In Friedman's view, central banks such as the Federal Reserve are obsolete. He proposed that the money supply grow by a rule-bound mechanism; banks should not be able to influence the money supply and would be as safe as possible; and the value of the dollar would be determined by the forces of world currency markets. Of course, if left completely unmonitored, such a system would soon break down because financial institutions would, by hook or by crook, find ways to engage in the equivalent of fractional reserve banking. Moreover, Friedman acknowledged that his policies would not end boom-and-bust cycles. In short, banks and other financial institutions still could fail, much to the detriment of regional and national economies and perhaps even the global economy.

Like Friedman, the so-called Austrian economists—Ludwig von Mises, Murray Rothbard, and Friedrich von Hayek, among others— also were staunch advocates of market forces. As such, they had nothing against financial concentration per se, provided that it is driven by market forces, not by decree or corrupt practices. They opposed government interference in the marketplace to the point of calling for the replacement of government fiat paper with the liabilities of private issuers and/or commodities. They were naturally suspicious of government regulations, especially those, like the safety net, that subsidize financial institutions, particularly large ones.

Without clear evidence of scale or scope economies, the Austrian economists view increased financial concentration with skepticism. Indeed, von Mises went so far as to assert that natural monopolies are "limited to some minerals . . . and to . . . local limited-space monopolies." Because many recent mainstream economists have had difficulty showing the existence of significant scale economies in financial services, the Austrians, like Friedman, want to eliminate or reduce regulations as well as the safety net. It seems to me they have it backward, at least when it comes to financial services. But the point here, again, is that no reputable economist argued for both deregulation and the too-big-to-fail doctrine, because the two views are logically incompatible.

Each of these leading economic thinkers, then, carefully considered the question of banking concentration. To be sure, through the centuries economists have given much greater attention to concentration among manufacturing firms than among financial institutions. But from Adam Smith forward, nearly every influential economist examined in this chapter recognized the special character of banks—especially central banks—and advocated some form of oversight or regulation to prevent abuses. The two exceptions, at opposite ends of the ideological spectrum, were Karl Marx (who was happy to allow a banking monopoly, provided it was owned and operated by "the people") and Milton Friedman (who preferred to let market forces rather than public officials safeguard the public interest). All the others were concerned that, in a capitalist system, leading banks held the potential to harm society, whether by monopolizing power or by taking on excessive risk. These are the enduring issues. What has changed, beyond the imagination of any of these great minds, is the scale and scope of banking concentration.

# 10

# Do We Still Need
# Glass-Steagall?

Throughout the post–World War II decades, financial regulation was dismantled piece by piece, and the pace accelerated in the 1980s. Back in 1987, when I was asked to appear before the Board of Governors of the Federal Reserve System on the merits of additional proposals, I cautioned that continuing a piecemeal approach posed significant risks. Rather, what was needed was comprehensive reform that took into account key structural changes in financial markets.

The need for a new regulatory framework that will encompass today's modern financial world with its global dimensions was great then, and is even greater now. We also need to strengthen our financial system and protect the safety of savings in our society, promote economic growth with a greater emphasis on equity rather than debt, and bring asset evaluation into the real world by eliminating many accounting fictions and omissions in the measurement of assets.

Back in the mid-1980s, some within the financial community petitioned Congress to dismantle long-standing regulatory structures. I argued before the Federal Reserve Bank of Kansas that it would be a serious mistake for lawmakers to analyze and resolve these applications on the basis of technical factors, such as percentage limitations asserted to be consistent with the "principally engaged" standard. On the contrary, I said, they should consider whether such proposals were consistent with the Glass-Steagall Act and the Bank Holding Company Act, and whether they would enhance the functioning of the financial system.

When Congress originally enacted these statutes, it made certain basic social policy choices regarding the necessity of separating commercial banking and investment banking, the structure required to limit financial risks, and the value of a decentralized financial system. However, interpretations of the Glass-Steagall Act in recent decades by both private financial participants and regulatory authorities have been aimed mainly at circumventing the Glass-Steagall Act's restrictive language, thereby permitting a variety of financial activities asserted to be in conformity with the new world of finance. Regardless of the merits of changes proposed, it would be a mistake for various regulatory bodies to approve or disapprove them on an ad hoc basis. Over time, that would create a financial system fundamentally different from that envisioned by Congress and one that, in my view, would usurp the legislative function of Congress.

I readily acknowledged in the mid-1980s that sweeping changes had taken place in the financial world—both in banking and in nonbanking institutions. Indeed, the pace of such developments has accelerated dramatically in recent years. The magnitude of these changes is, in fact, a principal reason why I believe the choices that the Federal Reserve Board has been asked periodically to make more properly belong to Congress. What is really needed is a careful and comprehensive reexamination of the problems and alternatives resulting from the developments that have taken place, and then the devising of a framework for an efficient, well-run, and disciplined financial system.

A brief review of just a few of the radical changes our financial system already was experiencing underscored the need for a comprehensive rather than a piecemeal restructuring of our financial markets. First, we were witnessing a blurring of distinctions among financial institutions.

The globalization of securities markets, long heralded, was unfolding with great speed. Our financial system was generating huge amounts of debt while failing to create an adequate amount of equity capital. At the same time, the system was fostering a massive proliferation of financial instruments and new trading techniques. The risk that these instruments entailed was neither known fully nor regulated adequately. To be sure, allowing commercial banks access to underwrite and trade an enlarged menu of open-market credit obligations might directly benefit the commercial banks themselves. But I believed it would accelerate debt creation, weaken further our financial framework, and increase the risks for economic stability.

The seminal issue was this: Should the Federal Reserve approve these applications for increased deregulation, thereby accelerating the process I have just described, or should it recognize that a piecemeal approach to the expansion of banking powers would have significant adverse effects that would overshadow any incidental benefits coming from approval? In my view, the answer was clear: Nothing short of a comprehensive approach to reform would resolve, rather than exacerbate, current problems.

I proposed a comprehensive overview for another reason. Many of the financial changes to which I refer had been taking place in the non-banking sector of our financial system, and any significant changes in the regulatory framework obviously would affect that sector. Specifically, an evident and important consideration in bringing about a new financial framework would be to ensure competitive equality among the different types of financial institutions involved, the so-called level playing field. Approval of the applications then under consideration would not have achieved this result because of the wide disparity of benefits, powers, and protections that existed among various institutions. To attain a level playing field, a number of prerequisites would need to be met.

First, financial assets held by banks would have to be valued and reported at the lower of cost or market, thus reflecting actual weaknesses and risks in a bank's structure, whether derived directly or through a securities affiliate. Bank capital would then have real meaning and value.

Second, the safety net of governmental protections and powers that exclusively benefits banks—and by this I mean Federal Deposit Insurance Corporation (FDIC) coverage and access to the Federal Reserve discount window, the Federal Reserve wire, and the direct payment system, as well as the perceived regulatory backstop that protects large banks from failure—would need to be either eliminated or made available to all major financial participants on equal terms.

Third, additional capital safeguards would have to be imposed to reduce the level of overall risk in the banking system. Capital regulations that fully integrate off-balance-sheet exposures and reflect the nature and risk of bank activities would be essential, as would the elimination of so-called intangible capital, which is a regulatory accounting fiction.

Policy makers also would be required to grapple with the question of whether the concerns I have just expressed can be met if securities activities are placed in a subsidiary of a bank holding company that would operate on an assertedly independent basis. Whether this approach was viable would depend both on the amount of autonomy granted to the securities affiliate and on whether the securities affiliate was truly free to fail.

It is not realistic to conclude that such an affiliate could somehow stand alone and be separate from its holding company parent or affiliated banks. As bank regulators have witnessed, problems at a subsidiary can easily spread throughout the holding company family and, more important, throughout the banking system, if only by a weakening of public confidence. Therefore, this linkage requires bank holding company managements to support all subsidiaries when they come under pressure. Ultimately, the holding company, affiliated banks, and, most important, regulators would have to stand behind a shaky securities affiliate.

Another major objective in fashioning a new financial system would be to eliminate, or at least minimize, conflicts of interest. An obvious conflict may well materialize where the same or affiliated entities are both lenders and underwriters for a commercial company. In my judgment, safeguards against these conflicts, though often proposed, cannot be fully adequate. It is also not valid to argue that potential improper relationships are present in virtually all buyer-seller relationships; rather, these problems are likely to be particularly acute in the context of a banking holding company with an incentive to cross-sell its products among its diverse customer base.

Another significant issue was the extent to which further concentration of economic power in a smaller group of entities would be harmful to our economic future and thus run directly counter to the intentions of the Bank Holding Company Act and to the competitive system.

In terms of competitiveness and innovative capacity, the U.S. financial system is unique. In European and other countries with universal banking, the capital markets are widely perceived as both insufficiently developed and inefficient. The concentration in the financial industries of these countries is quite high. Predictably, the spawning of new enterprises through innovative financing techniques and the access to diverse sources of funds is limited. Public debt and equity financing on behalf of all but the largest companies is difficult in Europe, and most financing transactions take place in a negotiated banking market. As a result, the banking and public securities markets do not have sufficient interplay to serve as truly viable competitive alternatives, offering financing flexibility and interest savings to public and private borrowers.

In view of these major policy concerns, I firmly believe that the issues raised by those who seek further dismantling of financial regulation need a conscious political solution, rather than an accidental, jerry-built result that is the sum of a series of fragmented regulatory decisions. Because the problems are so complex, however, before Congress is asked to act, the issues involved should be examined, and recommendations should be made, by a national commission designated by Congress and composed of financial regulators, representatives of the banking and securities industries, and distinguished private citizens. We should resist the further blurring of distinctions within the U.S. financial services industry, as well as the eroding of international financial borders. The myriad of financial regulators, which we have inherited as a vestige of past financial developments, has become incapable of governing a system where formal distinctions among types of institutions are rapidly disappearing.

# 11

# *Banking and Commerce Should Not Merge*

B y the end of the 1980s, most of the barriers separating various financial businesses had been dismantled. That was not enough for some advocates of deregulation, who sought to remove the long-standing barrier separating banking and commerce. I opposed such merger when I testified before Congress in May and September of 1991, and I continue to oppose it today. I believe it ultimately puts in jeopardy the fundamental economic democracy of this country and undermines the crucial need for independent deposit institutions exercising objective credit judgments.

A merger of banking and commerce would tend to produce an undesirable concentration of economic and financial power, while providing no significant compensating benefits. Ownership and control of banks by large commercial and industrial firms are not necessary for attracting needed new capital into the industry, even for troubled banking institutions that have a reasonable chance of restoring their viability. What is necessary is to rebuild investor confidence in the financial health and profitability of deposit institutions over the long term.

Such confidence has been severely impaired in recent years, which has been the most difficult period for the banking industry since the 1930s.

Banks, savings and loan associations, and other financial institutions, including insurance companies, have been confronted with extraordinary credit problems that must be overcome before they can fully restore their basic financial soundness. Under these difficult circumstances, it is easy to understand why many deposit institutions have found it hard to raise capital in the open market. But as they move to strengthen their balance sheets and put in place risk controls to prevent a recurrence of imprudent lending, the capital markets will respond positively.

A necessary precondition is to deal with the apparent failure of the regulatory system to anticipate and forestall this outburst of excessive lending, whether to risky real estate ventures or to dangerously overleveraged companies. The collapse of the Federal Savings and Loan Insurance Corporation (FSLIC) and the recurrent warnings that the Federal Deposit Insurance Corporation (FDIC) may also be in danger of insolvency are an important element. But the problem of the deposit insurance funds is by itself only one of a number of serious weaknesses in the financial regulatory system. There needs to be fundamental change in this area before banking, which is appropriately a regulated industry, is seen to be a good place to invest.

It would be unfortunate if the Administration and the Congress shied away from the arduous work of forging a compromise program of comprehensive regulatory reform that will permit deposit institutions to recover and prosper and that will rectify those regulatory weaknesses that permitted the lending mistakes of recent years. Settling for what might be a short-term expedient for recapitalizing the deposit insurance funds would be insufficient and could be counterproductive, to the extent that stopgap measures might further worsen the value of the banking franchise.

If farsighted, comprehensive reforms are made, however, once the process of rehabilitation of troubled institutions is well along, I have no doubt that many banks now excluded from the capital markets will be able to return. Over the longer term, a sound, profitable banking industry will normally have no trouble attracting both equity and debt capital in satisfactory amounts without the direct ownership and control of commercial and industrial firms.

Rather than merely criticizing what others had proposed, in 1991 I put forward a 10-point program for improving the functioning of our financial system. I believed this approach not only would lay a foundation for attracting capital to the banking business, but also would strengthen our nation's ability to achieve satisfactory noninflationary growth in the coming years. Some are proposals I had advocated for some time. Others were new. But together they outlined an approach that I believed was workable and capable of gaining broad support within the industry.

First, a National Board of Overseers of Financial Institutions and Markets should be established by Congress. This proposal, which I first made to the Congress in June 1985, goes well beyond the limited consolidation of supervisory responsibilities proposed by the U.S. Treasury. Let us recognize the fact that distinctions among groups of financial institutions are rapidly shrinking. Their markets are not as segmented as they used to be. They often compete directly for funds in highly interest-rate-sensitive markets and employ the same new financing and investing techniques. To continue to keep the responsibility for supervision divided along the segmented lines of institutional groups fails to recognize the reality in today's marketplace.

Among other things, this Board of Overseers could serve to bring together an integrated overview of our major financial institutions and markets. It should promulgate minimum capital requirements, uniform accounting standards, and procedures for disclosing greater income and balance sheet information. It should also tighten the responsibilities of the senior management and directors of institutions. All supervisory responsibilities should eventually fall within its jurisdiction. Membership on the Board of Overseers should include representatives from the Federal Reserve System and from relevant government agencies, and a select number from the private sector.

Second, a Board of Overseers of Major International Institutions and Markets should be organized by the industrial nations. The need for such an international board comes from the fact that international flows of funds are increasing as a result of debt securitization, investor preferences, and the rapid advancement in communications and the dissemination of information. If credit is to enhance rather than to destabilize international economic life, then the function of overseeing the rapidly changing international credit structure will have to be improved. Currently, this responsibility lies mainly in a cooperative arrangement among central banks. This is inadequate. Similarly to the proposed domestic board, the international board—which would consist of central banks and other governmental and private sector members of industrial countries—should set minimum capital requirements for all major institutions; establish uniform trading, reporting, and disclosure standards for open credit markets; and monitor the performance of institutions and markets under its jurisdiction.

Third, we must attract highly competent people into the official supervisory and examining functions dealing with markets and institutions by offering much higher compensation and by the setting of higher standards. The great importance of these assignments should be well publicized, and achievements in this area need to be widely recognized. It is unfortunate that the emphasis on deregulation during the 1980s relegated these responsibilities to a second and third level of importance.

Fourth, nationwide banking should be authorized. The Treasury is right that permitting nationwide banking is long overdue. The fragmented banking arrangements in the United States reflect our historical financial roots but not what is required to finance the modern, interrelated commercial, industrial, and financial society we now have. Today, there are no more significant pockets of captive savings. Our money and capital markets reach into all regions of the country and are closely linked internationally. Major credit cards and mutual funds are national and international in scope. Differences in financing terms among regions of our country have been systematically reduced through the securitization of debt and de facto national banking operations. It no longer makes any sense, if it ever did, to retain legal barricades whose only substantive effect is to hamper efficient deposit banking.

I would be opposed to nationwide banking if it would result in massive banking concentration that would establish monopolistic positions. But in the current circumstances that will not happen. This is because many of the very large money center banks are short of capital and still have a substantial volume of marginal assets to write down. They do not have the financial capacity to participate in banking consolidation.

Therefore, what is likely to emerge is an increased number of large banks. That top tier will consist of the existing money center banks, together with the largest regional banks and thrift institutions that have already been rapidly expanding, and a new group of well-capitalized regional institutions that have not yet aggressively pursued acquisitions. A reduced, but still substantial, number of small and medium-sized deposit institutions with special competitive strengths will also survive and prosper alongside these nationwide franchise builders. In all, banking competition will remain lively, and banking concentration ratios will be far short of what they are today in such industrial countries as Canada, the United Kingdom, and Germany.

Fifth, deposit insurance in the United States should cover all deposits and should not be restricted in size or number of accounts. This would maintain the value of the banking franchise and would not discriminate in favor of the banks that are considered too big to fail. The insurance risk can be substantially held down by requiring all insured deposit institutions to achieve over the next five years a credit rating from the official supervisors that is equivalent to AA in the open market. When an institution falls below this rating, it should be required to provide detailed plans for regaining the AA rating within the next year. With improved official supervision, few institutions would fall from the AA rating to a very marginal position and, to keep an AA rating, institutions could not abuse the use of brokered deposits. Moreover, the too-big-to-fail doctrine could be scrapped because all insured institutions would have to follow more conservative practices.

Sixth, well-capitalized commercial banks should be allowed to underwrite securities, but under stern restrictions: To avoid conflicts of interest, financial institutions involved in the underwriting of securities should not be allowed to underwrite securities for firms in which they have a direct stake, whether an equity position, a bridge loan, or a variety of loans if the underwriter is a commercial bank. An underwriting institution cannot exercise objective due diligence for the securities to be distributed to the public when the proceeds of the offering will pay off the loan in the institution's own holdings. Even disclosure of such positions is an insufficient check on potential abuses.

Seventh, all major financial institutions should be required to value their assets at the lower of cost or market. Being able to get a full and realistic account of the true financial position of a deposit institution will have a lasting positive effect on the willingness of investors to place fresh capital into the industry.

Valuation at lower than cost or market would be a vast improvement over the lax accounting standards of recent years, but it is also different from mark-to-market accounting as proposed by some others. My approach would require institutions to recognize losses quickly and put pressure on institutions to follow prudent practices. It would also enable deposit institutions to enlarge their capital by building up valuation reserves, without tax consequences, when values rise, thus rewarding those who have managed well and disciplining those who have done poorly. While some may claim that not all assets can be readily priced at market, this alleged shortcoming is overstated today. More obligations are now marketable than in the past, and expertise in official supervisory agencies should be developed to provide realistic valuations for the rest.

Admittedly, financial institutions have weakened balance sheets today, so the transition to this more exacting standard will take time. But at a conceptual level, opposition to this more conservative approach is shortsighted.

It is unduly apprehensive of how the markets will react to any negative earnings report. And those who oppose conservative accounting fail to appreciate the ongoing benefit to the strength of financial institutions and to the integrity of the entire financial system.

Eighth, I further believe that financial institutions should be required to report in far greater detail than at present both their profit achievement and their true financial condition. While the growth of balance sheet assets and liabilities of financial institutions has slowed in recent years, off-balance-sheet items—such as letters of credit, interest rate and currency swaps, or futures and forward contracts on currencies and securities—have continued to swell. In some cases they have reached magnitudes many times the size of reported assets and liabilities. The true rate of return on assets is actually overstated at present unless some fraction of these off-balance-sheet risks is folded in when appraising reported footings.

Ninth, I strongly endorse the principle of early intervention by regulators when a bank is going bad. Regulators should have a clear legal mandate to intervene in the resolution of a weakening institution while it still has some tangible net worth. This will help protect the taxpayer and it will send the right message to managers of financial institutions. But I would go further to support earlier intervention. That is, in my view financial regulators should have the clear legal authority to force changes in management practices that jeopardize a marginal financial institution's future capital position. Thus, the authorities should enforce tough restrictions on dividend payments by financial institutions with weak capital positions. Moreover, they should also have the authority to demand that managements restrict their own bonuses and other extraordinary compensation whenever that remuneration is based on short-term earnings performance. Too often, highly risky credits have been approved just to generate high fees that could be used to beef up current earnings and therefore executive compensation, but have left a legacy of credit exposure that has subverted long-term financial health. This myopia should be halted.

Finally, to enhance equity capital and to reverse the highly leveraged position of both commercial businesses and financial institutions, I recommend that the government eliminate the capital gains tax for investments held over one year and also rewrite the corporate income tax laws to do away with the double taxation of dividends. Both measures would tend to encourage a healthy switch from debt to equity finance. Both measures would also bring the United States into conformity with the practice in major industrial countries abroad.

The financial system that would result from this program would be one that fulfills all of the fundamental requirements for safety and soundness. It would have independent institutions that would be exercising objective credit judgments, weighing their fiduciary duties against their legitimate desire to make profits, disclosing fully their financial positions on the basis of realistic and conservative accounting principles, and operating under strict but reasonable regulatory standards developed with an eye to both domestic and international market conditions. It would be a financial system that buttresses the economy and supports business enterprises during periods of temporary stress. But it would not be a system in which commercial and industrial firms owned and controlled banks.

# PART IV
# FINANCIAL CRISES

# 12

# Postwar Financial Crises, 1966–2001

During my long career in the financial markets, which has spanned more than five decades, I've had a front-row seat to dozens of minor and several major financial crises. Fortunately, none of these upheavals lasted as long as the collapse of the 1930s, when roughly a third of the nation's financial institutions collapsed and many others barely functioned. There have been no fewer than 15 periods of major credit disarray that have affected the United States since World War II, as itemized in Exhibit 12.1. The first took hold in the 1960s, and no decade since has been free of travail. Some of these crises centered on events and institutions in the United States, while others originated elsewhere but were propagated within our system through its financial institutions. Several centered on individual institutions, while others were more systemic. To be sure, the functioning of U.S. financial markets and institutions in the second half of the twentieth century seems placid compared with the dramatic ups and downs of the previous two centuries. Yet it is quite remarkable that—in spite of remarkable progress in the exact sciences—our financial markets and institutions continue to be plagued by turmoil and uncertainty. What, then, can we learn from the previous half century's financial upheavals?

**Exhibit 12.1** Major Credit Crises from 1945 to the Present

| Year | Highlight | Comment |
| --- | --- | --- |
| 1966 | Credit crunch | Disintermediation. |
| 1970 | Pennsylvania Central Railroad failure | Overdependence on commercial paper issuance. |
| 1974 | Franklin National Bank failure | Foreign exchange speculation by borrowing heavily in Eurodollar interbank markets. |
| 1979 | Silver crisis | Large silver positions of Hunt brothers financed by Wall Street. |
| 1982 | Failure of Drysdale Government Securities, Inc. | Excessive use of repos. |
| 1982 | Failure of Penn Square Bank | High loan concentration in energy field. |
| 1982 | Mexican bailout | American banks were large lenders with a substantial amount due within one year. |
| 1984 | Bailout of Continental Illinois Bank | Financed Penn Square and others in energy. |
| 1984–1985 | Savings and loan crisis | Aggressive lending and investing. |
| 1987 | Stock market crash | Program trading. |
| 1989–1991 | Thrift bailout and commercial bank lending excesses | Junk bonds and takeover financing. |
| 1995 | South Korea and Mexico | Excessive short-term indebtedness. |
| 1998 | Malfunctioning of Long-Term Capital Management and Russian debt moratorium | Excessive leverage. |
| 2000 | High-tech bubble | Excessive stock valuations. |
| 2007-2009 | The Great Credit Crunch | Subprime mortgage crisis and overleveraged financial system. |

Financial crises not only upset financial institutions and markets, they undermine the economy. This is because their role in today's national and global markets is both critical and indispensable. To perform their roles well—to keep the wheels of commerce and industry spinning smoothly—financial institutions must balance their private interests with broader social and fiduciary responsibilities. We entrust them with our savings, short-term and long-term. We rely on them to allocate credit to households, to businesses, and to government. At the same time that they perform their fiduciary responsibilities as custodians of these funds, financial institutions are propelled by an entrepreneurial drive to grow and profit. Sometimes, however, entrepreneurial risk taking overwhelms the restraint demanded of fiduciary responsibility. When that happens, the result is volatility, economic dislocation, or, at worst, financial crisis.

As noted earlier, the consequences of a severe financial and economic crisis can be far-reaching. A major crisis can lead to fundamental shifts in political power, and—if long and deep enough—it can threaten economic democracy itself.

As I described in the Introduction to this book, I was profoundly influenced during my formative years by what I saw in the United States when my family emigrated here in the late 1930s to escape Nazi persecution. Economic recovery came after the Second World War erupted in Europe and Asia in 1939, when the U.S. economy began to mobilize to support its Allies. In Europe, the war was inspired in large part by financial upheaval: crippling hyperinflation in Weimar Germany helped pave the way for Hitler's lunatic dictatorship, which promised to restore order and national pride.

To fight the war, the United States borrowed heavily through a series of patriotic war bond drives, ran enormous budget deficits, and inflated its currency, though not as much as during the First World War. But after the war ended in 1945, the federal government quickly retired most of its debt and restored the economy to near equilibrium. Many Americans feared a return to depression, but this "depression psychosis," as economist John Kenneth Galbraith dubbed it, was short-lived. Soon the United States entered the greatest period of expansion in its history. It was a heady time for economic policy makers, most of whom believed they had unlocked the secrets of the business cycle. They spoke confidently of "fine-tuning" the economy and of "soft landings." And for a time it seemed they were right. During the eight years of the Eisenhower administration

(1953–1961), there were three relatively mild recessions. President John F. Kennedy embraced the increasingly popular Keynesian doctrine to stimulate the economy with deficit spending and tax cuts, a policy pursued even more aggressively by Lyndon Johnson, who in 1965 scaled up the Vietnam War when the economy already was running at near full capacity. Wall Street enjoyed a great bull market in the 1960s, buoyed by a number of glamour stocks in high-tech industries such as chemicals, pharmaceuticals, and electronics. As car owners cruised their new interstate highways, the automobile industry employed, directly or indirectly, one in seven American workers. Would the good times ever stop rolling?

The first significant postwar financial crisis erupted in 1966, triggered by two events. First, deposit institutions were drained of deposits because interest rates rose above the rates they were allowed to pay on savings and time deposits. The maximum rates that deposit institutions were allowed to pay were set by the Federal Reserve through a directive known as Regulation Q. Second, funds were withdrawn from life insurance companies because many of those policies allowed the policy holder to borrow at a low rate on the cash surrender value of the insurance policy.

By the summer of 1966—when the market hit the maximum allowable interest rate on large-denomination certificates of deposit (CDs)—the credit crunch was in full swing. For financial insiders, it was an extraordinary and scary event, especially given the mild rhythms that had prevailed since the end of the war. Households reduced their holdings of savings deposits and used the proceeds to purchase higher-yielding market obligations. The severe credit tightening had enormous ramifications for the housing market by forcing a wave of loan denials. It also squeezed businesses, many of which began to turn from banks to the open credit market to finance their expansion. Major financial institutions of all kinds—but especially the thrifts—liquidated their bond portfolios.

From my perch at Salomon Brothers, I had a firsthand view of this credit squeeze. Traders began to widen the spreads between buy and sell prices. Salespeople found it harder and harder to place new offerings. And the firm's own inventory of securities became increasingly expensive to finance.

Each day seemed to bring new—and more unpleasant—revelations. Three-month U.S. Treasury bills climbed to the lofty postwar height of 5⅝ percent, a rate not unusual now but unheard-of at the time. Southern California Edison, a stalwart utility, issued a long bond that yielded up to 6.19 percent in the secondary market. Many thrifts came under increasing pressure from deposit withdrawals. Large commercial banks, which began to experience problems in rolling over maturing certificates of deposit, scrambled to recoup by acquiring Eurodollar deposits and by issuing commercial paper through bank subsidiaries and affiliates.

Government action helped quell the crisis. In late August, the Federal Reserve issued a letter to the nation's commercial banks urging them to slow the growth of business loans and the liquidation of securities. It also indicated that it would tighten lending through the Fed discount window used by member banks. Around the same time, President Johnson called on federal credit agencies to curtail their financing and promised to trim the federal budget.

The leaders in business, finance, and government drew differing lessons from the credit crunch of 1966. Business corporations sought ways to avoid being constrained the same way in the future. Many entered the market as new issuers of commercial paper domestically and of bonds in the Euro market. Financial institutions such as banks and thrifts clamored for an easing of Regulation Q restrictions. For their part, individual investors began to reconsider their investment options. The credit crunch, by introducing thousands of small-scale investors to alternatives to ordinary passbook savings, provided the first glimpse of the dramatic democratization of investments that was about to dawn.

It is important to note that, throughout this crisis, credit quality remained high. In that significant respect, the 1966 crisis differed from

subsequent postwar financial upheavals, in which credit quality deterioration would figure prominently. The reason was that in 1966, the
denial of credit came quickly. Interest rates were halted from escalating
even further by financial market segmentation, by interest rate ceilings
imposed on banks and on thrifts by the government, and by competition with the capital markets themselves.

Still, the upheaval of 1966 left an indelible mark on American
finance. And it added new terms to the finance lexicon: *disintermediation*
and *credit crunch*. Sidney Homer, to whom I reported in my early days
at Salomon Brothers, did not coin the term *disintermediation*, as some
believed, but I believe that we did introduce into financial markets the
term *credit crunch*.

The next crisis hit in May 1970. The backdrop for this crisis reflected
some fascinating economic and financial conditions. In an environment
of rising inflation and wages, the Federal Reserve raised interest rates.
The federal funds rate climbed from 4.6 percent in 1968 to nearly 9
percent by the end of 1969. In addition, the Federal Reserve increased
reserve requirements by 0.5 percent in April 1969, primarily to dampen
inflationary expectations. The consumer price index, which had averaged 4.3 percent in 1968, had risen to 5.2 percent in the first half of
1969. But the Fed refused to raise the Regulation Q ceiling on large
negotiable certificates of deposit. Again, open market interest rates rose
above the maximum rate payable on time deposits in 1969. And again,
the banks were forced to accept a runoff in deposit liabilities, this time
exceeding the runoff in 1966.

Even so, large banks found sources of funds that partially mitigated
this pressure. First, they sharply increased their borrowing from foreign
banks, especially from their overseas branches, which in turn attracted
funds from the Eurodollar market. Second, many large banks had formed
one-bank holding companies that were able to issue commercial paper.

The proceeds of this issuance were used to buy loans from the banks. Third, the banks increased their reliance on the purchase of federal funds and the use of repurchase agreements (repos).

In this way, the banks for the first time in the post–World War II period made strong efforts to escape the restraining influence of monetary policy. The Federal Reserve eventually countered by requiring that member banks count outstanding drafts due to Eurodollar transactions as demand deposits subject to reserve requirements. In addition, money raised from repurchase agreements was subject to reserve requirements. These actions did eventually slow the growth of bank credit.

In the financial markets, constraints were gradually enveloping business. Corporate profits were falling while the cost of borrowing reached new highs for the postwar period. Short-term corporate borrowing was increasing rapidly, especially through the issuance of commercial paper.

In the then-tiny research department at Salomon Brothers, I brought my concerns about an increasingly likely credit crisis to my senior colleague, the great interest rate historian and money and bond market analyst Sidney Homer. Arthur Burns—a prominent economist of business cycles, Columbia University professor, and former chairman of the Council of Economic Advisers—recently had been confirmed as the new chairman of the Federal Reserve. Sidney had known Burns for many years, and suggested that we meet with him to convey our concerns about the credit markets. Burns had not taken possession of his Fed office, so we met the evening before Thanksgiving in 1969 in his State Department office, where he had been serving as a special assistant to President Nixon.

According to the data we showed the incoming Fed chairman that day, the volume of commercial paper in circulation had spiked up sharply in recent months. That, combined with the surging volume of bank loans, was undermining the quality of corporate credit and posing risks to corporate solvency. In the five years since June 1965, our data showed, commercial paper had multiplied by a factor of four, from $10 billion to $40 billion. Even though Burns understood our analysis, he didn't appear to share our sense of urgency about the credit explosion, and even if he had, there was not much he could have done at the time.

The credit crisis that Sidney Homer and I anticipated broke in the spring of 1970. As with most financial crises, this one was set off by the collapse of a single major institution, in this case the sprawling Pennsylvania Central Railroad. Already swimming in $200 million of commercial paper, the railroad saw no way to refinance soon-to-mature bonds and commercial paper. Its impending demise roiled financial markets and pummeled the Penn Central's share price. When Commercial Credit and Chrysler Financial, two of the nation's leading credit companies, found it difficult to roll over maturing commercial paper, pressure on the markets became intense.

In the midst of this turmoil, I was given another opportunity to offer high-level advice. The chairman of the New York Stock Exchange, Bernard "Bunny" Lasker, asked to see me the day before he was to meet with President Nixon to discuss the credit crisis. My advice to Lasker was that the president should encourage the Federal Reserve to lift some of the ceilings on time deposits and to ease monetary policy, both of which would improve the liquidity of the constricted credit markets. If Lasker could meet with the president privately and without press fanfare, all the better, I added. Lasker welcomed the advice, but ultimately proved unable to arrange a private meeting under the press radar or to speak completely frankly with the president.

Even so, the crisis abated several months later when the Nixon Administration and the Fed took the kinds of measures I had recommended: suspending the interest rate ceiling on some large-denomination certificates of deposit, which encouraged banks to issue a large volume of new CDs, and easing monetary policy. To fill the gap caused by the shrinking volume of commercial paper, banks expanded their lines of credit to corporations. And, indeed, the trend continued as corporations attempted to avoid a repetition of the early 1970s credit squeeze. But as commercial banks issued more and more loans with floating interest rates, financing them with borrowings and loans with similar maturity dates, they found themselves in the business of spread banking—a business that posed its own kinds of risks.

The next financial crisis—precipitated by the collapse of Franklin National Bank in 1974—brought the risks of spread banking into plain view. Here is how the crisis unfolded. Taking advantage of the relaxed ceilings on CD rates, Franklin heavily issued negotiable CDs and federal funds, while borrowing heavily in the Eurodollar interbank market. But the bank sustained large losses in the foreign exchange market—which in turn caused a private West German bank (Herstatt) to fail—as well as from many of its loans, because of their poor credit quality. The debacle roiled the markets for Eurodollars and foreign exchange, and further widened the spreads between CDs and Treasury bills.

The Franklin National crisis also marked a new era in American finance that went largely unnoticed. As Franklin and then Herstatt threatened to collapse, the U.S. Federal Reserve—seeking to minimize the damage in broader markets, especially the trade in CDs, and thereby to stabilize foreign exchange and Eurodollars—quietly stepped in and lent money to Franklin National. For the first time, the central bank acted as a lender of last resort in the international arena. It was a harbinger of the future.

Speculative financial activity came to the fore in the late 1970s and the 1980s through the silver crisis in 1979, the failure of Drysdale Government Securities and the Penn Square Bank, and the 1982 debt crisis in Mexico. The silver crisis involved the Hunt brothers, who had cornered the silver market by borrowing huge amounts on margin. By the first quarter of 1980, the Hunts' obligations totaled roughly $1.75 billion, partly owed to banks and to the well-known securities firm Bache & Company. Loan renegotiations and asset sales by the Hunts ultimately alleviated the problem.

Drysdale got into trouble through massive repurchase agreement (repo) operations that ballooned its assets and produced profits until shifts in market conditions prompted participants in the repo arrangements to limit their activity. Penn Square, domiciled in Oklahoma, became illiquid because of its rapid loan growth, a high proportion of which was concentrated in the energy field. The threat of a Mexican debt default seemed imminent by the summer of 1982. Of the $80 billion of outstanding Mexican debt, $25 billion was owed to U.S. banks, a large portion to the nine largest American banks. Such a loss would have substantially endangered the capital position of these large banks. And the fact that this debt was denominated in U.S. dollars complicated the Mexican task of servicing the debt; Mexico would have found little relief from floating the Mexican peso in the currency market. Conditions eventually stabilized after a restructuring of the Mexican debt was worked out among 100 banks from around the world. The U.S. government and the International Monetary Fund (IMF) provided new credit facilities.

Domestically, the crises of the 1980s were in large part the result of aggressive lending and investing practices by thrift institutions. This, in turn, was fueled by the newly enacted Depository Institution Deregulation and Monetary Control Act of 1980, and even more directly by the passage of the Garn–St. Germain Depository Institution Act of 1982. These laws allowed federally chartered institutions to expand their lending in nonmortgage activities such as the consumer and business credit markets. The institutions also branched out into adjustable-rate mortgage financing and into mortgage-backed securities. The impact of the new congressional legislation was quick and clear, as liberal lending and investing practices proliferated.

I also watched those developments with great interest at Salomon Brothers. On one of my trips to the West Coast, I had a breakfast meeting with Tom Spiegel, the CEO of Columbia Savings and Loan, located in Los Angeles. He was very enthusiastic about the sizable position his company was taking in junk bonds. From his perspective, investment in these obligations would reduce his operating overhead. He saw the credit quality of junk bonds as being in many ways comparable to that of mortgages, and was encouraged by the apparently sound credit quality assessments on the obligations made by outside vendors. I raised what I thought were serious questions, especially about Mr. Spiegel's reliance on the street analysis of credit risk, but these were brushed aside. Sadly, Columbia Savings and Loan failed in 1990, a year after my visit.

Another example of 1980s excesses involved the Financial Corporation of America (FCA), the holding company of American Savings and Loan, a client of Salomon Brothers. FCA was pursuing an aggressive growth strategy. This involved, in part, the heavy acquisition of mortgage-backed bonds from Salomon Brothers through repurchase agreements. The savings and loan (S&L) would buy the bonds. Salomon would finance the acquisition, while the buyer was required to put up only a small equity margin and a promise to unwind the transaction within a week or two. The S&L would earn the difference between the yield on the underlying mortgages and the financing cost it paid to Salomon Brothers. For its part, Salomon would benefit from the difference between its own borrowing costs and the interest payment made by the S&L. On the surface, this repo arrangement was very profitable to Salomon. We actually charged the S&L 50 basis points above the traditional repo financing rate. Eventually, these repo arrangements came to total nearly $2 billion.

I had three reservations about transactions of this kind. First, repos were traditionally designed to accommodate very temporary financing needs. The repo with this S&L was rolled over at maturity with no indication as to when it would be closed out. Second, there was the question of whether we could legally seize the collateral in the event the S&L got into trouble. Third, even if we could seize the collateral, I suspected it would be very difficult in deteriorating market conditions to liquidate the underlying obligations. Sure enough, FCA became mired in financial difficulty. Salomon was fortunate to have liquidated the repo just in time.

In the midst of the speculative financing activity highlighted by the issuance of junk bonds and liberal lending by the thrifts, the stock market crashed on October 19, 1987. The Dow Jones Industrial Average fell by 508 points, or 22.7 percent. Prior to the crash, the Fed had tightened monetary policy in response to inflationary pressures and dollar weakness in the foreign exchange markets. In September, the Fed had raised the discount rate to 6 percent, and on the eve of the crash the funds rate stood at 7.6 percent. But the rate hikes seemed to have little impact. In the first half of 1987, the stock market rose more than 26 percent, and continued to gallop right up to the October crash.

In searching for the mechanism that triggered the crash, many experts focused on a technique called portfolio insurance. Considered a hedging device, portfolio insurance used profits made in the futures market to offset losses incurred on the stocks held in the actual portfolio. This required very complex computer programs that would automatically execute programmed trades.

Meanwhile, the bond market had been transformed by the so-called junk bond revolution, the brainchild of Drexel Burnham Lambert's wunderkind Michael Milken. Before the 1980s, the market for junk bonds—which were rated below investment grade—was tiny. Corporate bonds in that category accounted for only 13 percent of outstanding publicly traded issues. But a study by Brad Hickman under the auspices of the National Bureau of Economic Research published in 1958 showed that lower-quality corporate bonds generally turned in a reasonable price performance, even factoring in losses from default. This was the insight that Milken seized on; he saw junk bonds as a lucrative opportunity because, selling for much less than investment-grade bonds, they would attract many new investors into the bond markets. The strategy worked, earning a fortune for Milken and his firm, which quickly dominated the high-risk bond market and as late as 1986 commanded about 40 percent of that market.

During the 1980 junk bond boom period, I was very much disturbed about the impact it would have on financial markets and especially its influence on the direction of Salomon, where I served on the firm's executive committee. To be sure, the profits from this business were high. There were high underwriting fees, and trading spreads in the secondary markets were very wide. At the same time, there were conflicts of interest. These were aggressive placement efforts for new issues, and the research department came under intensive pressure to issue favorable reports on new junk bond issues and on outstanding obligations. Junk bonds were frequently used to finance corporate takeovers. At Salomon, increasing efforts were under way to challenge Drexel's junk bond supremacy. These efforts were taken under the guise of moving into higher-profit-margin activities and deemphasizing lower-profit-margin business. I disagreed with this approach, and ultimately it was one of the determinants that led me to resign in April 1988. Subsequently, Drexel Burnham Lambert failed and Mike Milken was indicted and sent to jail.

The new decade rested on a somewhat wobbly foundation of junk bonds and dubious real estate investments. Junk bonds remained the rage, their yields climbing from 13.6 percent in 1987 to 19 percent at their peak in 1989. By the early 1990s, quite a few major financial institutions—from pension funds to foreign institutions to giant insurance companies—held portfolios thick with junk debt as well as real estate loans of questionable credit quality. And several major mutual funds held outstanding bonds (liabilities) fixed at 600 to 700 basis points above the yield on comparable U.S. government bonds. The result was another major credit crunch, which the Fed took too long to acknowledge and alleviate through monetary easing. The economy began to recover in late 1993.

But the decade's travails had only begun. The initial wave of problems was international: the Mexican peso crisis in 1995, the collapse of the Thai baht in 1997, the South Korean debt crisis in 1997, and the Russian debt default in 1998. The core problem was that the countries involved had borrowed too heavily in international debt markets.

In quite a few instances their borrowings involved obligations denominated in foreign currencies, especially in U.S. dollars, and a heavy proportion of it was concentrated in paper with short maturities. Prominent financial institutions were generally involved as underwriters or lenders or both.

With the notable exception of Russia (which defaulted on its debt), the IMF, the United States, and other key industrial countries successfully stepped in to relieve the debt problem. There were good reasons for these financial leaders to assist. Systemic turmoil in global financial markets was in no country's interest. For U.S. banks, debt moratoriums and defaults would require losses and write-offs that could hurt balance sheets. In the case of Russia, large direct financial aid was not an immediate antidote, but an easing of monetary policy, especially in the United States, may have helped indirectly.

The Russian debt default also contributed to the troubles of Long-Term Capital Management (LTCM) in the summer of 1998 because LTCM had Russian bonds among its holdings. The history of Long-Term Capital Management was well chronicled by Roger Lowenstein in his book, *When Genius Failed*. I nevertheless want to add some personal observations, because I was there when this hedge fund was not yet organized but rather was in its embryonic stage. The key organizers of LTCM came from Salomon Brothers, where some had blossoming careers when I was a senior partner and member of the firm's executive committee. Prior to John Meriwether's arrival, Salomon periodically did some proprietary positioning of securities. They were taken on an opportunistic basis. For example, the firm might trade a large block of common stock and retain a portion in its own portfolio to achieve a long-term gain. The same approach was sometimes taken through the retention of a portion of a large bond trade. There were a few exceptions to this approach. In one such rare instance, the firm invested a moderate sum for its own account in oil exploration. One such investment with Paul Haas was exceptionally profitable. None of these activities were undertaken on an organized and departmentally managed basis.

Market developments and the arrival of John Meriwether at Salomon Brothers changed all that. In the market, more marketable obligations were created, and derivatives started to play a role in trading and in the positioning of securities. The Arbitrage Group, which was formed in 1977 and headed by Meriwether, formalized the proprietary effort. It was the precursor to LTCM and to the proprietary trading that other firms eventually initiated and that became a focal point for Goldman Sachs.

Even in those early, pre-LTCM years, a few of my partners and I noticed several disturbing aspects of this new Arbitrage Group that later would plague the hedge fund. For example, it was exceedingly difficult to limit the positioning of the Arbitrage Group. For quite a while, these positions involved standard convergence trades, the shorting of one security against a long position of another security with both having the same maturity. This seemed simple enough until the maturity on the obligations became longer or differed somewhat in credit quality. Occasionally, these transactions would tie up a significant amount of the firm's capital and would limit our trading positions in dealing with our traditional clients. That produced occasional frictions with other parts of the firm. This somehow was tolerated because the Meriwether group with a relatively small number of people was generating a substantial volume of profit. Indeed, this issue of the size and variety of risk taking was at the heart of the trouble that LTCM suffered later on. It also seemed to me, at least, that the Arbitrage Group did not fit well into the culture of Salomon Brothers, with its tough trading and aggressive salespeople who were steeped in the give-and-take of a noisy and at times boisterous trading room. In contrast, many of the key people in the Meriwether group had advanced academic degrees, were trained in quantitative risk analysis, and fraternized primarily with their own group. Their success was a sort of achievement that might be called "the revenge of the nerds." Nevertheless, their success and pressure were noticeable in a shift toward attempts to internalize more of the activities of the firm.

From my perspective, the key developments that led to the demise of LTCM in September 1998 were the following:

First, there was an unwillingness to set limits to total risk taking. That management weakness had surfaced earlier when a key trader in Meriwether's Arbitrage Group while still at Salomon took positions in a U.S. government auction beyond legal limits.

Second, there was the deep and growing conviction that risks could be readily quantified regardless of maturity, credit quality, or country of origin of the security. That approach gained public credence, at least in the minds of the investors in LTCM, with the involvement of three financial luminaries: Robert C. Merton, probably the leading scholar at the time in finance; Myron Scholes, who was well known as the co-author of the Black-Scholes formula for option pricing; and David Mullins, a former vice chairman of the Federal Reserve Board.

Third, belief in the capacity to quantify risks encouraged a massive leveraging by LTCM. At the onset of difficulties in September 1998, LTCM had capital of $3.6 billion and an involvement in the derivatives markets with a notional value of more than $1 trillion.

Fourth, the lenders to LTCM were not aware of the total financial involvement by LTCM in the financial markets. Their failure to perform adequate due diligence was motivated by the huge volume of trades that LTCM would bestow on them if the credit accommodations were liberal. In many instances, therefore, the sale and trading departments, with the blessings in some instances of the senior management of the lending institution, did not pay adequate attention to the warnings that may have been issued by the credit analyst of the lending institution. The substantial profit that could be gained over the near term was too compelling. LTCM neatly exploited this incentive to the maximum.

Fifth, the official supervisors and regulators failed to recognize what LTCM had created in the financial markets—its huge relationships with many of the key money market institutions in the United States with whom it was involved as a debtor though a vast array of transactions. When financial markets came under greater price pressures in the summer of 1998, putting the risk modeling by LTCM in temporary disrepute, and LTCM experienced a large capital loss, the Federal Reserve stepped into the breach to broker a deal between LTCM and its major creditors, the major money market institutions, thus avoiding a systemic risk.

Surprisingly, the LTCM debacle was quickly forgotten. As noted in the next chapter, many of the attributes that contributed to the LTCM fiasco were very much operative in the crisis that surfaced in 2007. By that time, proprietary trading had become the key component of many of the large financial conglomerates. They not only emulated LTCM but also expanded the scope of this risk-taking activity.

As the 1990s came to a close, markets were again roiled, this time by the opening wedge of what became known as the great dot-com meltdown—the collapse of a nearly two-decade run-up in high-tech stocks, many of them issued by companies that never posted tangible earnings. Between August 1982 and March 1999—when the Dow closed above 10,000 for the first time—the index had climbed more than 1,000 percent. Earlier that year, the dollar volume traded on the young (1971) tech-heavy NASDAQ Composite index had exceeded that of New York Stock Exchange for the first time in history. In spite of a series of Federal Reserve rate hikes, the Dow set a new record (11,477) on December 28, 1999. As in other periods of market euphoria, some pundits proclaimed a new era of endless expansion, and wrote books with fantastical titles such as *Dow 36,000* and *Dow 100,000*.

The Federal Reserve under Alan Greenspan seemed at a loss for how to cope with the runaway bull market. Greenspan's occasional tepid attempts to talk down the market seemed only to introduce volatility. The NASDAQ broke the 5,000 mark in March 2000, but that same month the Dow fell below 10,000. The Fed boosted interest rates to 6 percent, but market volatility continued through April and May. The Internet stocks that had propelled the run-up were by now taking a drubbing. Lucent Technologies, descended from the nation's stalwart "widows and orphans" firm, AT&T (aka Ma Bell), saw its market value plummet $32 billion after the company announced quarterly earnings three cents below expectations. Several newer publicly traded companies lost from 90 percent to 98 percent of their market value. In the year ending March 2000, the NASDAQ fell 62 percent, while the Dow was down thousands of points.

The dot-com meltdown, like most of the postwar financial crises before it, was largely a story about credit markets gone awry under the eyes of a half-asleep central bank. In this case, venture capitalists funneled billions of dollars of capital into firms without performing traditional due diligence. Rather, they accepted a so-called new economy set of measures such as "clicks" and "eyeballs" (referring to the number of web site visits) rather than assessing return on equity, earnings per share, and other more traditional measures. Venture capitalists and tens of millions of ordinary investors paid dearly when the bubble burst.

For its part, the Federal Reserve had become prisoner to the wealth effect—the massive run-up in share prices that was boosting household confidence and, in turn, helping to propel consumer spending. If the Fed acted too aggressively to stanch the bull market, the reasoning went, the larger economy was likely to suffer. The question is, wouldn't the consequences have been less severe if the bubble had never expanded to begin with?

A number of common threads run through the financial upheavals that preceded the current crisis, which is the subject of the next chapter. First, with the exception of the 1966 credit crunch, all involved an excessive use of credit. Second, each was accompanied by a discernible lowering of credit standards. Third, investors had come to rely heavily on leverage prior to each postwar crisis. Fourth, each crisis also was preceded by a period of market euphoria. And, finally, although each postwar financial crisis inspired some modest regulatory reforms, the overall trend in the past half century has been toward the greater and greater liberalization of financial markets in ways that have tended to tip the balance in favor of irresponsible risk taking.

The interest rate setting surrounding the post–World War II crises was not uniform and was rather diverse. From a broad perspective, the first four crises occurred during a period when interest rates were still rising secularly. The great secular bear bond market had started in 1946 when long U.S. governments were yielding 2½ percent and ended in 1981 when they reached 15¼ percent. All of the rest materialized while a secular bull bond market has been underway in which the long U.S. bond fell below 4 percent in the first decade of the new century. One conclusion that can be drawn from the observation is that credit crises can occur in both secular bull and bear bond markets.

It also should be noted that in most instances, it was not a tough monetary policy that induced the bursting of the credit bubble. Instead, it was a sharp deterioration in the credit situation. Such developments as speculative lending and investing and recourse to high leverage eventually caused market relapses. For example, these developments were behind the sharp increases in junk bond yields from 1987 to mid-1991, from 1998 to mid-2000, and from mid-2004 to early 2008.

# 13

# The Great Financial Crisis of 2007–2009

The current credit crisis—with its epicenter in the U.S. mortgage market—is the most serious upheaval in the American financial markets since the end of the Second World War. Although the current crisis shares many characteristics with the other postwar crises I reviewed in the previous chapter—indeed, it is in many ways the culmination of structural trends long in the making—it also is a particular confluence of institutional and behavioral forces, including new attitudes toward debt, market opacity, and the central role of financial conglomerates in the world's leading money capitals.

The mortgage market has seized up. Credit quality yield spreads have widened dramatically, reflecting great uncertainty concerning the prices of many financial assets. Asset write-offs by large and prominent financial institutions have been huge and, in the period since World War II, unprecedented. The fifth largest investment bank was nearly forced into bankruptcy, which, in the final hour, was averted through a sale to JPMorgan Chase brokered by the U.S. Treasury and the Federal Reserve. Two key government-sponsored agencies—Fannie Mae and Freddie Mac—were bailed out by the federal government. Lehman Brothers failed. The common stock of financial institutions has fallen precipitously. Many major institutions have sold large blocks of shares to replenish their equity capital positions. Meanwhile, a large number of smaller institutions, lacking adequate access to open markets in order to alleviate strains on their capital, face the likelihood of being taken over by the Federal Deposit Insurance Corporation (FDIC).

All this dire institutional news has severely dampened banking and investing activities, which surely will delay economic recovery. When recovery finally comes, the financial crisis will leave a deep imprint on investor behavior and on our financial institutions.

In my book *On Money and Markets*, published nearly a decade ago, I called attention to a number of structural changes in our markets that—if they were not recognized and controlled by policy makers— would lead markets to dangerous extremes. Since then, these changes have become even more prominent, and are in fact many of the driving forces behind the latest crisis. They include the very nature of the securities in which credit is denominated, the ways credit is valued, the ways instruments are traded, the ways financial institutions are managed, and the complexity of today's giant financial conglomerates. Many of these same structural changes contributed to previous financial crises, as noted in the previous chapter, but they have not been appreciated fully within the investment community until recent years.

The current financial debacle has brought the structural changes transforming our financial markets into full view. At the center of these trends has been the massive creation of debt, which has far outstripped earlier excessive periods of credit creation. Exhibit 13.1 shows that nonfinancial debt exceeded nominal gross domestic product (GDP) by nearly $19 trillion in early 2008, compared with $8 trillion in 1999, $4 trillion in 1989, and only $500 billion in 1979.

These exhibits provide at best a partial glimpse of what happened in recent years. It is difficult to exaggerate the scale and scope of financial market expansion in recent decades. By any measure, current financial activity—whether new financing or trading volume—dwarfs past volumes. Indeed, we do not have data that accurately measure the full

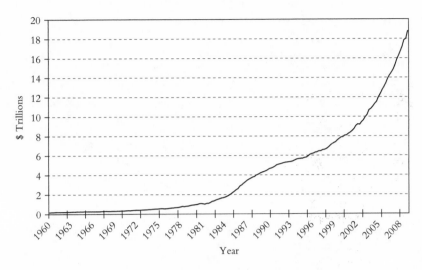

**Exhibit 13.1** Outstanding U.S. Domestic Nonfinancial Debt Minus Nominal Gross Domestic Product, 1960–2008

magnitude of what is going on. Long-standing traditional credit instruments, such as stocks, bonds, and money market obligations, have been joined by a long and diverse list of credit instruments, many of which are extraordinarily complicated. Here are just a few examples to illustrate the feverish pitch of financial activity. As shown in Exhibit 13.2, the notional amount of global exchange-traded derivative markets rose from $60 billion in 2000 to $530 billion at the end of the second half of 2008.

Credit default swaps increased from $632 billion to $54.6 trillion during this period (see Exhibit 13.3).

And the pace of trading was frenzied. The turnover volume on the New York Stock Exchange, summarized in Exhibit 13.4, catapulted from 78 percent in 1999 to 123 percent in 2007. Stated differently, the daily average volume of transactions in 2007 was nearly 2.5 billion shares, up from 800 million in 1999.

One major contributor to the feverish pitch in financial activity was a new understanding of liquidity among market participants, which gained momentum in the waning decades of the twentieth century and

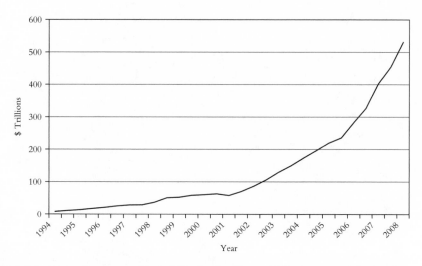

**Exhibit 13.2**    Exchange-Traded Derivative Financial Instruments: Notional Principal Amounts Outstanding, 1994–2008

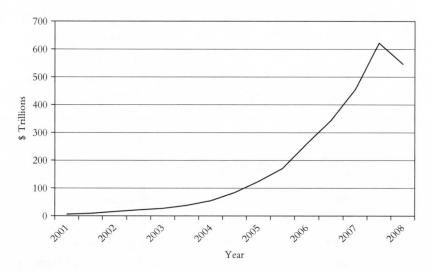

**Exhibit 13.3**    Credit Default Swaps: Notional Principal Amounts Outstanding, 2001–2008

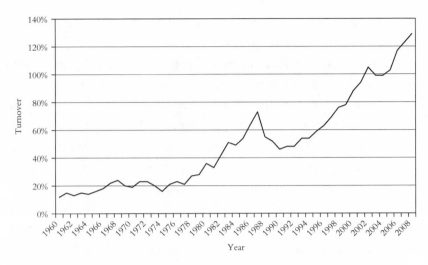

**Exhibit 13.4**  Annual Percentage Turnover of Stocks Listed on the New York Stock Exchange, 1960–2008

came into full bloom in recent years. During the post–World War II decades, liquidity was by and large an asset-based concept. For business corporations, it meant the size of cash and very liquid assets, the maturity of receivables, the turnover of inventory, and the relationship of these assets to total liabilities. For households, liquidity primarily meant the maturity of financial assets being held for contingencies along with funds that reliably would be available later in life. In contrast, today firms and households alike often blur the distinction between liquidity and *credit availability*. When thinking about liquid assets, present and future, it is now commonplace to think in terms of *access* to liabilities. Money matters but credit counts.

That change in the perception of liquidity in just a few decades is extraordinary. I still recall the great joy felt by homeowners when they made the final payment on their mortgage. Some families even had mortgage burning parties. Many heads of household still harbored vivid memories of the Great Depression, and so welcomed the day they could own their property outright. But as the postwar economic boom rolled on, traditional, conservative attitudes toward household debt increasingly gave way to more expansive views.

For corporate financial management, the shift toward a very liberal approach to liquidity is equally startling, and played a key role in the latest credit crisis. From 2001, when business recovery began, to the end of 2007, corporate profits rose sharply from $767 billion to $1.642 trillion. But in spite of the accumulating earnings, corporate credit ratings decreased in greater numbers than they increased. Corporations leveraged themselves more and more, through a combination of new borrowings and share repurchases, while at the same time paying dividends at rates that outstripped new retained earnings. They were, in short, overly generous to shareholders while plunging deeper into debt.

There are a number of other distinctive features that make the current crisis special. First, unlike many previous postwar financial upheavals, which were centered in emerging markets, this one is playing out in markets and institutions in the world's leading financial centers, chiefly in the United States and Europe. In that way, it is striking at the heart of the global economy rather than damaging its limbs. Second, closely related to this observation is the fact that this latest crisis is heavily centered in large financial institutions. Third, the credit instruments implicated in the current crisis are supposedly *tradable*, whereas in the past they often were nontradable. That difference has compounded the current problem because the predominance of the marketable obligations has made the credit crisis more readily *contagious* throughout the global economy. Fourth, it is more difficult now than during previous credit crises to assess the real magnitude of the problem. This is because in recent years, markets have become increasingly *opaque* rather than more and more transparent, as is widely believed. Fifth, much of this opaqueness flows from the fact that our financial system is larger, more complex, and more interconnected than at any time before, and that the dominance of behemoth, integrated financial firms makes it nearly impossible today to accurately gauge risk exposure. These financial conglomerates dominate financial markets both here and abroad far more than at any previous time since World War II.

**What Went Wrong?**

**Mr. Okonogi:** What went wrong, causing this gigantic financial crisis?

**Dr. Kaufman:** There are several mistakes. Our monetary supervisory officials did not recognize this problem early on. They recognized the problem too late and their response to it was a little bit at a time rather than decisive.

Back in May or June, or even last year, the chairman of the Federal Reserve Board [Ben Bernanke] said that the subprime mortgage problem was contained. Well, it wasn't contained. It became a bigger and bigger problem.

If you go back, the main failure by the Federal Reserve and others was to fully understand what the implications would be for the financial markets from the structural changes that were occurring in them.

What was meant, for example, by the creation of securitization? What implications did it have for supervision and regulation? What were the implications for financial markets and for the economy, for example, from the rapid growth of derivatives? And how should these markets be supervised and regulated? What were the implications of financial institutions becoming financial conglomerates?

And as you know, today a bank is not a bank. An insurance company is not an insurance company. An investment bank is not an investment bank. Many of these are under an institution called a "financial conglomerate."

Citigroup, Inc. today is not just a commercial bank. It's many different things and it's in many different markets. Our supervisory authority, our monetary authorities did not fully appreciate what those structural changes would mean for the behavior of financial market participants and what the implications would be for the economy.

"Crisis Certain to Lead to Major Deficit Spending," interview with Kiyoshi Okonogi, *Asahi News*, November 15, 2008.

Finally, against this backdrop is the troubling fact that some of those who manage leading financial institutions and markets have seriously lapsed in some significant ways. There are several key players in this story. There are the directors and senior managers of large financial institutions, many of whom have failed repeatedly to implement policies that would assure that risk taking is kept within reasonable bounds. There are also the private credit rating agencies that are, it seems to me, overwhelmed by the enormity of their task and might be hobbled by conflicts of interest. Then there are federal financial regulators, which have consistently failed to probe deeply enough to uncover dangerous credit and risk practices. The Federal Reserve—the primary guardian of our financial system—has not appreciated the extent to which profound structural changes in the financial markets have demanded new and different monetary policies and practices. The failure looms large as a contributing factor in the current crisis.

Consider the conundrum of increasing securitization with market opaqueness rather than market transparency. Opaqueness has been on the rise largely *because* of the explosion of securitization (that is, the conversion of nonmarketable assets into marketable obligations) in recent decades. Economic theory suggests that securitized markets operate on the basis of accurate prices and accurate assessment of credit quality, which are readily available to all market participants. Obligations are supposed to be analyzed objectively by credit rating agencies and by those underwriting and trading them. And these mechanisms of information and control supposedly have been strengthened by an array of new credit instruments that mitigate risk taking, most notably financial derivatives. Meanwhile, the securitization revolution has been undergirded by a host of sophisticated new quantitative techniques that, according to those who employ them, can define risk probability with very high levels of precision.

The motive to securitize, while failing to assess risk properly, is at the same time quite powerful. And as those two lines diverged—the scale and scope of securitization, and the willingness and ability of market participants to assess risk properly—securities markets became more and more focused on short-term returns. Financial intermediaries quickly perceived the expansive profits to be gained through securitization. There were opportunities aplenty, ranging from managing the securities of others to underwriting, distributing, and trading freshly commodified obligations. As one commentator (David Smick) noted recently, "Securitization contributes one other huge weakness to today's financial system: The bankers who engage in lending are no longer tied to the risk of the borrower. The lender no longer has the incentive to avoid danger- ous risk at all costs because the risk, when cut up into pieces, is quickly shoved out the lender's door to be packaged with pieces of other risk, and to be sold as investment to the unknowing global financial commu- nity" (David M. Smick, *The World is Curved: Hidden Dangers to the Global Economy* (New York: Portfolio, 2008).

Because securitization extended even beyond nonmarketable assets such as mortgages and was truly global, the profit possibilities seemed, to many market participants, virtually unlimited. Given these com- pelling motivations, it is not surprising that securitization propelled credit creation and financial-market transactions to unprecedented heights. And, for nearly a decade, the near mania for securitization pro- vided generous rewards. Until the middle of 2007, U.S. financial profits outstripped those in broader markets. Profits in the financial sector leaped ahead from $151 billion in 1995 to $473 billion by mid-2007, a 313 percent increase, while the profit of all other sectors rose from $453 billion to $896 billion, or 197 percent, during the same period.

In some ways, it appeared that financial intermediation had become more important than the activities in the real world. While such a trend logically could not endure, the entrepreneurs of credit creation, nev- ertheless, looked forward to even greater riches. That was quite evi- dent from the expansion plans of the large financial conglomerates.

In general, these plans called for enlarging their participation in markets both here and particularly overseas and for increasing personnel.

In the past decade, technological change also has bolstered the easy-credit outlook now commonplace among investors. As markets have been linked globally by information technology networks, financial information flows nearly instantaneously, computerized trading is spreading, and transactions are executed almost without delay. Investors can access financial data and participate in markets around the world and around the clock.

These two developments—securitization and the seamless interconnectivity of markets—have brought intricate quantitative risk modeling to the forefront of financial practices. Securitization generates market prices, while information technology offers the power to quantify pricing and risk relationships. The potency of this combination—its effect on risk taking—cannot be overstated. Armed with complicated modeling techniques, increasingly powerful computers, and reams of historical market data, a growing number of investors have become entranced with the dream of scientific rectitude. Few recognize, however, that such modeling assumes constancy in market fundamentals. This is because it does not adequately factor in the future impact on prices of underlying structural changes, such as those I have been reviewing.

For many years I have questioned the efficacy of the overbearing reliance on quantitative risk analysis. Can these models take into account the impact of growing financial concentration in the making of markets and in the pricing of securities that are traded infrequently or that have tailor-made attributes? Can they truly quantify the risk to financial markets from a major military flare-up, from the ravages of a pandemic flu, or from a terrorist attack that would immobilize computer networks? And what about shifts in the broader monetary environment?

The growing popularity of quantitative investment modeling during the past decade or so has come at a time of very accommodating monetary policy. This raises the question of how risk modeling will fare in a more hostile monetary environment—for no one assumes that the monetary ease will continue forever. Albert Einstein clearly understood the problem associated with heavy reliance on quantitative techniques. In his office in Princeton hangs a sign that states, "Not everything that counts can be counted and not everything that can be counted counts."

# PART V
# POLICY FAILURES AND REFORMS

# 14

# Public Policy and
# the Markets

F iscal and monetary policies—key features of public policy—have a powerful and occasionally overriding influence on financial markets. They have a direct influence on the value of financial assets, the allocation of financial resources, the process of financial intermediation, the level of interest rates, and the rate of inflation, and thus on the behavior of the economy. The performance of both these arms of government has been far from perfect but not without accomplishments. There has been no repeat of the kind of economic depression that left such deep scars in the 1930s—an achievement for which public policy can claim some credit. However, there have been business recessions and significant financial mishaps.

For a good part of the post–World War II period, two approaches were in the center of public policy: Keynesianism and monetarism. The Keynesian view held that a flexible fiscal policy—one that is supposed to be in correct alignment with the needs of the economy—could be enforced by the political body. The much-heralded Kennedy tax cut in the early 1960s gave this approach considerable impetus. However, the unpleasant, disciplining side of fiscal activism, which entails the timely raising of taxes and pruning of federal expenditures, failed miserably in the subsequent years. Flexible fiscal policy as a means of stabilizing the economy was discredited further in the 1970s. Inflation picked up and the U.S. dollar came under attack in the foreign exchange markets. In the 1980s, an unprecedented wave of federal deficit financing took hold. Interest rates fluctuated widely, and the onslaught of a huge volume of new U.S. debt made it difficult for the Federal Reserve to tame inflation. Only in the latter part of the 1990s did fiscal policy seem to be in alignment with the needs of the economy. Large budget surpluses materialized. I believe, however, these surpluses were insufficiently incorporated into monetary policy decisions, which I will touch on in greater detail later on.

This is not to say that monetary policy has always distinguished itself. The monetarists, however, made considerable headway as inflation defied all attempts by the Keynesians to contain it. The targeting of the monetary aggregates came to the fore and reached its zenith in the United States when Paul Volcker briefly adopted a strict adherence to monetarism in October 1979 as a means for breaking the back of a virulent inflation that was then in progress. Before this attack on inflation subsided, the yield reached 17.5 percent on three-month Treasury bills, 15.25 percent on long government bonds, and 21.5 percent on the prime loan rate. Thereafter, monetarism as a policy technique gradually faltered as it became increasingly difficult to define money. Indeed, the Federal Reserve completely abandoned the targeting of money in 2001. Still, it took a long time before the Fed dismissed monetary targeting. This is because the Fed's preference has always been to allow the market process to evolve and not to interfere with it.

That approach, however, contributed to the Fed's inability to recognize early the impact that structural changes in the financial markets have had on financial behavior and the significance of these behavioral changes for the conduct of monetary policy. For example, the Fed did not fully grasp the ramifications from the lifting of the Regulation Q ceilings on time deposits to the point where banks were freed from this restraint by the 1980s. In fact, central bankers generally underplayed these banking changes on the enforcement of monetary policy.

With great flexibility in how they managed their assets and liabilities, financial institutions had become intermediaries, in the sense that they no longer had to bear the money rate risk. As long as these institutions could maintain a favorable spread between the cost of liabilities and the return on their assets, it no longer mattered how high interest rates were pushed by the monetary authorities. In their competitive zeal, many made weak loans and poor investments that eventually had to be written off. This new dynamic had serious long-range consequences. Because the relationship between the availability of funds and the demanders of credit had changed, interest rates now had to be driven up to extraordinary heights for the central bank to achieve a restraining effect.

The Fed also was slow to recognize the implications for monetary policy of an important related development: securitization. By and large, the central bank supported and encouraged the spread of this technique for turning nonmarketable credit instruments (such as mortgages) into marketable ones. Once again, the Fed welcomed an innovation that promised to increase the efficiency of financial markets, but did not put into place safeguards against potential abuses. In this case, the problem with securitization is that it tends to lower the standards for the granting of credit.

Like securitization, derivatives—which also multiplied rapidly in recent decades—encourage a more relaxed set of credit-granting standards. From a broad economic policy perspective, securitization has far-reaching consequences. The degree of credit restraint in operation at any particular time cannot be measured by standard money supply or bank credit indicators. Other time-honored rules of thumb—such as the notion that financial intermediaries are in the business of borrowing short and lending long—are being turned on their heads as well. Financial institutions engaged in active securitization may be borrowing long and lending short, while hedging their exposure to interest rate movements through a series of transactions in financial futures and options. In this new environment, surges in credit demands have not had the conventional effect of flattening the yield curve; the impulses are quickly transmitted up and down the yield curve through the actions of the new lending originators. In this way, greater volatility is transmitted to the intermediate-term and long-term bond markets, with corresponding effects on equity markets.

The Federal Reserve's slowness in perceiving the implications of these structural changes contributed to spawning quite a few of the crises in recent decades. The Fed has mistakenly assumed that the discipline of the market would sufficiently keep large problems from erupting.

Another unresolved challenge confronting the Federal Reserve involves the Fed's role as a lender of last resort. How far should the Fed spread its safety net? This is a nagging and rather messy issue in this rapidly changing financial world. The generally unstated assumption in years gone by was that the safety net should extend to the largest commercial banks that, after all, are the traditional wards of central banks. Whether there should be a lender of last resort for other types of financial institutions in order to avert a devastating shock to the financial system at large is not settled. Central bankers, of course, vehemently deny any such mandate in their public utterances.

Even in dealing with those traditional wards of central banks—the commercial banks—the issue has become very complicated. Commercial banks, in the traditional sense, are not commercial banks anymore; investments banks are not investment banks; and insurance companies are not insurance companies.

Large encompassing financial institutions have rather quickly come onto the financial scene. And as more such institutions are organized, more will be considered too big to fail. If so, the declining portion of the market that would be allowed to fail under this new setting will have to experience the real brunt of monetary restraint. Unfortunately, the institutions that are allowed to fail will enhance the market position of those that are too big to fail. Generally, the official view on this matter is that too-big-to-fail institutions are punished for irresponsible behavior. Lenders to such institutions may lose principal. Stockholders may suffer losses. Senior management may be dismissed. What tends to be overlooked is that the financial system is damaged by the excessive credit creation that occurs before the large bank is bailed out.

The other problem that confronted the Federal Reserve during the past decade was the role that the large swings in financial wealth should play in determining monetary policy. Unfortunately, the Federal Reserve did not become openly concerned about the wealth effect until late in the 1990s. By that time, stock prices had risen dramatically, speculation was rampant, and the volume of trading had skyrocketed, reflecting an increasingly near-term orientation by households and institutions in their portfolio behavior.

At first, the Federal Reserve responded to the stock market bubble ambiguously. In a speech back in December 1996, then Fed Chairman Alan Greenspan talked about the Fed's concern with rising stock prices. He asked: "But how do we know when irrational exuberance has unduly escalated asset values, which then become subject to unexpected and prolonged contractions as they have in Japan over the past decade? And how do we factor that assessment into monetary policy?" That expression—which got wide attention and was criticized by many— wasn't even a declaratory sentence. It was a rhetorical question.

The Fed's ambiguity in dealing with the stock market bubble was reflected again later on in July 1999 in congressional testimony by Chairman Greenspan, when he stated that "identifying a bubble in the process of inflating may be among the most formidable challenges confronting a central bank, pitting its own assessment of fundamentals against the combined judgment of millions of investors."

From another perspective, the Fed failed to appreciate the extent to which the huge expansion in private credit growth was fueling the boom in capital spending, consumption spending, and speculative finance. An extraordinary shift had taken place in credit demands that were hidden by the overall demand for credit. Credit demands rose on average just around 6 percent a year during the four years ended 2000. However, the demands of households were up 8 percent and those of businesses by over 10 percent, while the federal debt contracted by

**Why Henry Kaufman Is Worried**

I don't know of any period in the post–World War II years when the level of equity prices was so critical to the economic performance of the United States and that of the rest of the world [as now (1999)]. Now, there are those who believe that we are in a new world and that these values are somehow correct. I doubt that. There is no analytical, rational technique by which you can forecast the extreme of financial euphoria or the extreme of financial despair. But once despair in this market sets in, there is a real risk it could precipitate a recession—not only in the United States, but globally.

[Unfortunately, the Fed's position is:] "We don't know where there is a bubble, but once it is deflated, we know what to do." So the market is now somewhat conditioned. If prices go down, it expects the Fed to intervene. But it assumes the Fed will keep hands off as prices go up.

"Why Henry Kaufman Is Worried," *Barron's*, November 8, 1999.

nearly 3 percent. These were the credit ingredients that lifted stock prices and market exuberance.

Changes in the structure of the financial markets will continue to have profound influence on the way the economy interacts with the financial system and therefore pose some tricky problems for the conduct of monetary policy. The first problem is that a more open, deregulated, securitized, and global financial system will help keep debtors in the game longer than in times past. Securitization is a force for liberality in granting credit. Consider the recent case of South Korea. Here was a country that had made commendable progress toward transforming itself into a first-world country. It was undeniably an export powerhouse. The government did not run a large budget deficit. Outstanding external debt of the government was moderate. Credit ratings were extremely high. So the bankers—Japanese, European, and American—were willing to lend large amounts for short-term maturities, assuming that they could securitize those credits at will. Never did they give much weight to the possibility that the borrowers might be confronted with a liquidity crisis that would slam the door shut on access to the purportedly open credit markets.

Moreover, the rapid development of financial derivatives also perpetuates a more relaxed attitude toward granting credit. Higher-rated corporations can arbitrage their credit standing to lower their cost of funds by issuing long-term fixed-rate debt and then swapping the proceeds against the obligation to pay at a floating rate. Lower-rated corporations that would ordinarily be squeezed out of the bond market as the credit cycle matures are able to lock in long-term yields by borrowing short and swapping into the long-term maturity obligation. The bankers who are in the middle view their role as relatively risk-free.

A second problem for monetary policy is that the structural changes in the financial markets make conventional methods for anchoring monetary policy obsolete. Monetary targeting has been the initial casualty. The Federal Reserve continues to set target ranges for the rate of growth of several definitions of the money supply, but it goes to great lengths to assert that it doesn't take the targets very seriously because old relationships between money and the rest of the economy have become entirely unreliable. That is true also for measures of credit. Securitization is associated with a diminished role of depository institutions in the intermediation of credit flows, and so debt aggregates are just as unreliable as monetary aggregates. Paradoxically, while private sector institutions are increasingly relying on mathematical models in the quantification of risk, the central bank is shying away from a quantitative approach to conducting monetary policy.

What are the choices? There are not many. A central bank can do as the Bank of England has done and condition policy on meeting an intermediate-term inflation target. Or a central bank can set an inflation target and to try to attain it by pursuing a formal monetary conditions rule, along the lines of how the Bank of Canada is operating. Or it can do as the Federal Reserve has been doing, setting a loose and unquantified objective of "reasonable price stability" and using discretionary policy changes in pursuit of that goal.

But in each case the objective is cast solely in terms of the price indexes for goods and services. It explicitly leaves out any room for taking into account inflation (or deflation) of asset prices. But financial well-being depends on much more than merely attaining a low and stable rate of inflation. The proof of that is the case of the United States in the 1920s and that of Japan in the 1980s and 1990s. Both would meet any reasonable definition of price stability, but both suffered horrendous economic consequences from excessive asset price inflation followed by asset price collapses. Surely monetary policy should be not indifferent to such potentialities.

Wealth effects are now recognized to be powerful influences on the evolution of the economy. Not too many years ago, the Federal Reserve, as well as most other central banks, was somewhat skeptical about the potency of wealth effects. But today it is conceded that more and more households recognize how their financial net worth is affected by movements in asset values, and adjust their expenditures on goods, services, and housing accordingly. Business corporations modify their investment decisions in part in response to what is happening to their share prices. Business formation is subtly influenced by the level of the stock market, too, because a strong market allows individuals to take risks that they would not be inclined to take if the level of equity prices were substantially lower. International capital flows, and thus the value of the dollar, are also affected by the value of financial assets—and expectations for future asset price movements. Thus, these effects have become an important transmission belt from the financial sector to the real economy and necessarily a valid consideration for monetary policy.

While financial excesses and their hurtful economic consequences can never be fully eliminated, I believe they can be limited by improved supervision and regulation of financial institutions and markets. The modern, globalized financial structure is based on innovation and risk taking. Formal regulations and barriers to financial activities have been lowered, and over time they will come down further. Paradoxically, however, in a more deregulated, freewheeling financial environment, there is actually an *increased* need for better supervision of the financial institutions and markets. Equally important, there has to be more intensive and more informed market discipline of risk exposures, and that requires more information about what those exposures are. Oversight—whether by official institutions or by the market itself—has been uneven at best and usually tardy, with far too little information sharing among official organizations and far too little dialogue with private lenders and investors. Furthermore, in many of the emerging markets, formal regulatory mechanisms have been weak, and informal supervision and oversight has been practically nonexistent.

The essential ingredient in an improved global financial architecture is to establish a new institution, alongside a reorganized International Monetary Fund (IMF) and World Bank, to overcome the inadequacies of current national and international structures for supervising and regulating financial institutions and markets. To deal with the growing potential for market excesses, I have recommended many times over the years establishment of a Board of Overseers of Major Institutions and Markets to put teeth into the system. This Board would have the following three-part mandate:

1. It would set forth a code of conduct for market participants to encourage reasonable financial behavior.
2. It would supervise risk taking not only by banks and other financial institutions that have always been regulated and supervised, but also by new participants in the global markets.
3. It would be empowered by member governments to harmonize minimum capital requirements; to establish uniform trading, reporting, and disclosure standards; and to monitor the performance of institutions and markets under its purview.

Eventually, this new international regulatory body would rate the credit quality of market participants under its authority. Institutions that failed to abide by the standards would be sanctioned. Lending to banks in countries that choose to remain outside the new system would be subject to higher capital requirements and limitations on maturities. Also, nonmember countries would be limited in their ability to sell new securities in the equity, bond, and money markets of members. The new Board would not enact specific regulations to control flows of capital internationally, but it would visibly raise the bar to take advantage of the benefits of open capital markets. That will dramatically reduce risks in the system, although it will not eliminate them entirely.

At the same time that this new financial supervisory and regulatory entity is established, the IMF needs to be reorganized so as to perform competently a more targeted set of core functions. The new IMF, like today's IMF, would be responsible for organizing and partially funding emergency lending operations to protect the safety and soundness of the global system when member governments face intense balance-of-payment problems and are shut off from normal sources of external financing. It would continue to have the responsibility for setting policy conditions that borrowers must follow to qualify for emergency loans.

In contrast to present IMF practices, however, it would have the responsibility of anticipating problems and pressing member governments to take timely preventive actions. It would be responsible for rating the economic and financial strength of its members. It would evaluate their monetary and fiscal policies as well as the structures of their economies. Where it detected deficiencies that could lead to excessive dependence on inflows of short-term capital from abroad or could compromise the health of the domestic banking system, it would demand early remedial actions. If the member governments refused to act, the reorganized IMF would make the reduced credit rating public. Since that would of course have the effect of dramatically shrinking the recalcitrant country's access to the open credit markets, it would represent a powerful incentive for the member to cooperate.

Rating the creditworthiness of sovereigns is a tough job, but an appropriately staffed IMF would have a far better chance of doing the job effectively than the private credit rating agencies, which are handicapped by a lack of the kind of the detailed and timely information that the IMF would be able to get.

Finally, it is imperative for the new European central bank and those of the United States and Japan to begin a dialogue on how to better harmonize their monetary policies. Each has to be prepared to recognize and take into account the global dimensions of what they do. If their actions end up creating an overabundance of global liquidity, there is a threat of either global inflation or excessive growth of global credit. If they end up with an insufficiency of global liquidity, economic growth may be jeopardized. It is probably too much to ask that this effort at better harmonization explicitly incorporate the goal of minimizing the huge swings in currency rates that have plagued the international monetary system in recent years. But there ought to be at least a systematic attempt to discuss the implications of outsized currency movements for the global trading system. Existing forums, such as the Bank for International Settlements (BIS) in Basel, Switzerland, are fine but too informal to achieve that systematic approach.

Why do official policy responses seem to lag so far behind structural changes in the financial markets? There are a number of reasons. One is that officials often underestimate the potency of a structural change. By the time it is obvious that something of importance has taken place, the development has triggered a series of market adjustments that are not readily brought under the official regulatory framework. A second is that structural changes do not always fall within the neat categories that delineate the various existing official institutions. For example, when financial derivatives emerged as a major element in modern financial markets, there was considerable uncertainty over where they would fit within the official regulatory apparatus. That uneasiness as to who should oversee financial derivatives has persisted, even as the market has been buffeted by several mishaps in recent years. A third reason why official policy responses lag behind structural changes in the financial markets is that at the early stages of a development, the impact of the changes on financial and economic behavior is difficult to quantify. To illustrate, the rapid increase in the public's investments in the equity market through the use of mutual funds was well documented. But it took quite a long time before U.S. financial officials appreciated how this phenomenon might generate a significant wealth effect for many millions of households. Now that the wealth-effect addiction has spread widely, policy makers are beginning to understand that the level of consumer expenditures on goods, services, and housing is intimately related to the strength of the stock market—and that there might be considerable withdrawal pains were the stock market to be set back dramatically.

Internationally, official policy responses to structural changes in the financial markets are handicapped by similar and other shortcomings. Vested interests in the official international financial institutions that may need to be reformed feel threatened by the unknown outcome of reform and tend to be vocal in their opposition. Moreover, there is the unwillingness to give up national sovereignty, even though financial markets and the economy are integrating globally. It seems, for instance, that the U.S. government is a reluctant proponent of a major overhaul of the current official international financial institutions. It may be that this is out of concern that any thoroughgoing reform might require the United States to yield some of its dominance over these institutions. If true, this would be shortsighted leadership, since there is no permanent benefit in being the dominant participant in an institution whose authority and credibility are being eroded by structural changes in the marketplace.

Finally, developing countries are said to be opposed to reform of official international financial institutions because they are afraid that improved scrutiny of financial institutions and markets would jeopardize their access to funds in the private markets. For instance, they may be concerned about the consequences of being impelled to improve transparency in their domestic banking system or otherwise bring to light financial problems that might otherwise have been kept out of sight. This is a terrible misconception. Retaining access to credit for less than credit-worthy institutions will only exaggerate the financial and economic cycle, as Asian nations have discovered painfully. What is in their interest is to reduce the extremes in financial cycles, because in so doing they would help produce a steadier and less interruptible flow of private funds.

Financial excesses eventually impoverish the marginal borrower and for a while at least mainly go to strengthen the bargaining position of the strongest participants in the credit system—namely, the governments, financial institutions, and business corporations of the major industrial countries of North America and Europe. That is certainly the clear message that comes out of the financial wreckage in Asia. Unfortunately, this narrow advantage is only a transitory benefit, since ultimately we all are losers as financial difficulties fan out from their origins. Thus, it is worth pondering whether the risks are already rising in our financial markets and whether we can avoid damage to our own economy in the absence of adequate official remedial actions to respond to the financial excesses that may now be percolating beneath the surface.

# 15

# *The Perils of Monetary Gradualism*

L
eading up to the current credit crisis, the U.S. Federal Reserve had moved toward a gradualist approach in its interest rate adjustments. Although many economists welcomed the policy shift, I have been concerned about the trend for several years. Back in 2004, for instance, I cautioned an audience at the Fifth Annual Community Bank Investor Conference in New York City (sponsored by Keefe, Bruyette & Woods) that monetary gradualism would lead to many unwelcome consequences, including an even greater debt overhang.

The Federal Reserve had just raised the federal funds rate ¼ percent to 1¼ percent. By itself, this small increase had very little significance. In fact, because of its minimal size, the bond markets breathed a sigh of relief and subsequently rallied, so that the immediate impact was to marginally ease rather than tighten credit conditions generally.

Nonetheless, in a broader context it marked a significant demarcation point. It was the first reversal in rates in over three years. And we knew back then that once monetary policy shifts, additional moves in the same direction tend to follow. Indeed, that is now the general expectation in the market. The consensus market view also holds that each of the increases in the funds rate will be of small proportion and not be introduced hurriedly. If it were introduced hastily, Fed policy would have significant implications for the economy and the markets.

What is the Federal Reserve trying to achieve? The textbooks would say that it wants to hold inflation in reasonable check by keeping financial resources in alignment with our economic capacity. It does this by raising or lowering interest rates on the premise that such actions will influence the flow of money and credit. In the first few decades following World War II, Fed actions to restrain got an assist from legal ceilings on deposit rates and on mortgage lending rates. These ceilings shackled the intermediation role of financial institutions, which were forced to restrict their lending and investing. This helped to restrain credit demands and interest rates. By the early 1980s, these restrictions were gradually removed. As a result, when the Fed tightened policy in recent decades, the cyclical peaks in interest rates were much more market-determined and occasionally flared upward rather dramatically. The peaks in interest rates very often occurred after demanders of credit borrowed much beyond their financial capacity. In the process, credit booms and/or speculative bubbles frequently materialized. It was in that more market-oriented environment that monetary policy makers found it difficult to ward off many financial excesses . . . with dire consequences.

The central bank has been extolling the virtues of this approach to monetary policy. The directives of the Federal Open Market Committee stress a policy of "measured response." This has been generally interpreted to mean that in the immediate future the Federal Reserve does not anticipate any developments that would require dramatic policy tightening actions. The underpinnings to this approach were described in great detail by Fed Governor Benjamin Bernanke in a 2004 speech entitled "Gradualism." The main tenets of a gradualist approach to monetary policy were set forth as follows:

First, central banks should move cautiously because of the uncertainties involving the underlying structure of the economy and of the impact that the policy change will have on the economy.

Second, by initiating small monetary actions, the Federal Reserve has the opportunity to evaluate the impact of its actions on the economy and markets and "to refine their views on how large a policy change will ultimately be needed."

A third reason for gradualism set forth by Governor Bernanke is that such a policy improves financial stability. It is supposed to allow banks to manage their assets and liabilities in such a way that will allow them to maintain profit spreads. This is supposed to reduce financial market volatility and risks of shocks to the financial system.

To be sure, economic and financial prospects are always difficult to project with a high degree of certainty. We all face that problem, whether we are in business or in government. Monetary policy is no exception. To pursue a policy of gradualism is a way of reducing the amount of judgment in the policymaking process. It also assumes that mistakes can be rectified with no or limited costs by adjusting policies when new information validates an event that already has occurred, such as an increase in inflation or a slowing in the economy.

Still, with this approach will there really be a catch-up to the underlying economic and financial forces, or will there be in train a policy of cumulative delays? Either too much or too little credit may still be injected into the economy with a gradualist policy. If so, how much monetary policy change is then required to return to equilibrium? No monetary formula can define what is then needed. Looking back, gradualism hardly has been error-free. History has shown that gradualism contributed to financial excesses in the past. Witness the events of the 1920s, and the delay in adequate monetary response in the 1970s and again in the second half of the 1990s. And there is little question that monetary gradualism helped foster the financial excesses that led to the collapse in 2007.

The measured response approach by the Fed is heavily influenced by its expectations that the inflation rate will be constrained by excess capacity to produce here and abroad. This is because of the increase in obsolescence due to rapid technological improvements. It is also important to recognize that China, which is already producing at a high level of its capacity, has in place policies to slow its rapid growth. Therefore, the downward pressure on the prices of goods exported by China should ease somewhat.

The gradualist monetary approach seems to have performed admirably for many years. The economy performed well early in the twenty-first century. Inflation was moderate. Back in 2004, when the policy was taking hold, the yield curve was sloped extremely positively. Viewing it from the conventional approach—that is, the yield differential between the 30-year U.S. government bond and the three-month Treasury bill—the differential was a positive 380 basis points. That was close to the high of a few months earlier, and since 1953 was exceeded only briefly in late 1992. It should be noted, however, the extreme positive slope in 1992 involved yields, both short and long, that were considerably higher than those prevailing in early 2004.

I believed at the time that it would take a considerable period before small increases in short rates would hamper business and households. Even a doubling or tripling of the level of the funds rate seemed unlikely to be too costly to borrowers or to make funds inaccessible. As I noted earlier, business corporations have a large capacity to finance in the short term. Households can increase their reliance on financing new housing through a variety of mortgages where the initial interest rate costs are still historically low. While both businesses and households will be taking on some interest rate risks, they will be comforted somewhat by the gradual pace of the rise in short-term rates.

Slowly rising short-term rates at the time of a steep yield curve generally do not discourage the many different carry trades in the market. The many value-at-risk analytical techniques encourage many participants to conclude that money risks can be calculated with reasonable certainty and that many profitable opportunities are available along the yield curve or at some yield spread from one market to another. In addition, monetary gradualism against a backdrop of a positively sloped yield curve nurtures still further the mushrooming speculation that underlies some of the activities in financial derivatives.

### The Fed's Narrow Focus on Core Inflation

**Ms. Schoenholtz:** The Federal Reserve tends to focus on *core* inflation, but U.S. policy makers have received some criticism on this front recently from observers, including from central bankers outside the United States. How do you judge that core inflation focus in a world where oil prices may be a reflection of global price pressures?

**Dr. Kaufman:** Well, I never really believed in these core inflation indexes. As you know, some of this got started when Arthur Burns, then the chairman of the Federal Reserve, was also confronted with a high rate of inflation, particularly in oil prices, so he wanted an index excluding oil. And then, of course, food prices went up very sharply, and the new core was made to eliminate food. So "ex-food and energy" was the approach, and that has more or less prevailed in the language of the Federal Reserve for some time.

The fact is that higher energy prices or higher food prices have to be financed, and then enough credit has to be put into the system in order to facilitate that. So, the Federal Reserve had facilitated (in that narrowly defined sense) higher energy prices. I think it's wrong. Energy is an important item in what we do in terms of using an automobile, or in the home, or in other activities.

So, I would strongly argue that we should use an encompassing kind of inflationary index. But even looking at the personal consumption expenditures (PCE) deflator, it is creeping beyond what perhaps the Federal Reserve deems as acceptable. Nevertheless, the Fed has made an indirect excuse for it, saying the economy will slow, and (therefore) as the economy slows over the next 12 months or so, perhaps we will see a moderation in these core inflation indexes. Well, that is on the basis of an econometric forecast, and life doesn't fully run on econometric forecasts.

Excerpt from "Talking with Dr. Henry Kaufman," Kim Schoenholtz interview with Henry Kaufman published in Citigroup's *Global Economic & Market Analysis*, October 17, 2006.

Now let me turn to the view that monetary gradualism improves financial stability and decreases the volatility of bank profits. These are highly laudable objectives, but they conflict with important realities. Today's financial institutions are geared toward expanding credit and innovating new credit techniques and instruments. They set near-term profit objectives that are supposed to motivate their operating staff to increase loans, investments, and trading opportunities. Where is the large conglomerate financial institution today that does not provide revenue and profit targets for the year ahead for each of its subsidiaries that are not above the levels achieved in the latest year? Monetary gradualism provides considerable support for this kind of targeting. As a result, credit creation continues to flourish, and its inflationary and destabilizing impact on the system is only recognizable with a delay.

The Federal Reserve continues to face a vexing policy conundrum. On the one hand, a gradualist approach can serve to bolster the economy. This is because of its favorable impact on financial asset values facilitated by the financial entrepreneurship I just described. While the Fed will not say that it has an explicit financial asset value in mind when it formulates policy, it surely has a close eye on stock prices, which, if they fell sharply, would affect economic expectations very adversely.

However, monetary gradualism also serves to increase substantially the American debt structure, which by historical standards is very high. For example, by 2004 the outstanding debt of U.S. domestic nonfinancial sectors was about double the magnitude of gross domestic product (GDP). By comparison, debt exceeded GDP by only 85 percent 10 years earlier, and by just 56 percent in 1984.

These concerns inspired me to state the following when I spoke at the Community Bank Investor Conference back in 2004:

> As one looks out over the next few years, one feature of the mounting private debt is particularly troublesome. It is the likelihood of trouble in housing. Housing prices adjusted for inflation have increased by nearly 50 percent in the past 10 years. In several areas of the U.S. the

increase has been even more dramatic. Real estate financing terms have become very liberal, and the objectivity of real estate appraisals has become questionable. We have already begun to see evidence that large numbers of households are overextended, with personal bankruptcies exceeding 1.5 million over the past year, double the number of a decade ago. Monetary policy has downplayed the risks of a real estate bubble just like it did in the 1990s when stock prices soared to unrealistic levels. Gradualism in monetary policy was not the right antidote at that time. Will it be this time around?

Unfortunately, we know how it turned out. I wish my deep concerns had been unfounded. But it seemed virtually unavoidable to me at the time that the next recession was a few years away, and would strike when debt was much higher. For that reason, it seemed imperative that monetary gradualism would have to be abandoned, because the heavy debt load of businesses and households would not be ameliorated by moderate monetary easing. Otherwise, I warned,

> The freedom of monetary policy to respond aggressively might also be circumscribed by the twin deficits that have been much talked about. Both the federal budget deficit and the deficit in our balance of payments would loom large. Political pressure to have a large fiscal stimulus to stem the recessions may be difficult to restrain and the foreign willingness to finance a large portion of it may wane.

The structural imbalances in our financial markets—ranging from the continued rapid growth of debt to the changing role and behavior of institutions and other participants—will not be addressed by monetary gradualism. These imbalances, however, continue to pose very serious challenges that must be tackled by a new monetary policy regime.

# 16

# The Fed and the Governance of Financial Institutions

The governance of financial institutions is a topic that has occupied center stage in business and finance in recent years. The main reason, of course, is the wave of abuses that has swept across the business and financial scene. These abuses have come in many forms and affected many institutions—from leading corporations and financial firms to private-sector regulators—but they share in common the corruption of rules and norms of behavior about good governance. And, unfortunately, I doubt we have seen the end of the unwelcome revelations.

How have we reached this state of affairs? And what can we do to begin to restore trust and confidence in our systems of financial governance?

We might begin by asking: Should we take any action at all? Why not let the unhampered marketplace determine outcomes? After all, the marketplace is supposed to reward and penalize: Winners profit, losers fail. At the core of undiluted free-market democracy is the belief that this process of winnowing out the good from the bad is ultimately fair, efficient, and essential for maximizing overall economic growth.

But, alas, we don't live in a perfect economic democracy. Such a notion is a theoretical construct. Ours is an imperfect economic democracy, one that applauds *competition* yet is uncomfortable with *failure*. Our system uneasily attempts to balance the benefits of competition with the virtues of social justice. And we try to temper the sometimes socially harsh effects of competition—most apparently, when it comes to very large institutions, both financial and nonfinancial. In our system, the largest institutions are deemed too big to fail.

These protected giants typically hold huge liabilities relative to their capital base and are interwoven with myriad other institutions and market participants through a complex network of asset and liability relationships. Given these interdependencies, the failure of one major institution can endanger the well-being of other intermediaries. These relationships therefore pose large but impossible-to-quantify risks for financial markets and for the larger economy. And because the "too big to fail" standard is likely to persist in our imperfect economic democracy, good governance in large institutions is especially critical.

In spite of the compelling need for such good governance at financial institutions, their history has been punctuated by many shocking lapses and excesses. In the Gilded Age of the late nineteenth century, Wall Street was regularly upended by the often successful attempts by colorful figures such as Daniel Drew, Jim Fiske, and Jay Gould to manipulate prices and corner markets. To be sure, there was virtually no formal regulation of the exchanges in those days; but financial markets depended on trust and ethical dealings no less than now.

Or consider the financial travesties committed during the speculative days of the late 1920s, which resulted in far-reaching legislation that constrained (probably to an excessive degree) the activities of many financial intermediaries. Before that landmark legislation was passed, Congress interrogated many of Wall Street's most prominent figures. The interrogations were often acrimonious, and some of the most shocking revelations of those days have a curiously contemporary ring. Consider this account of investment banking abuses from the 1920s, as described by Ferdinand Pecora, the counsel for the Senate Committee on Banking and Finance, in his book, *Wall Street Under Oath*:

> This was the origin of the famous so-called "preferred lists," whose publication stirred the nation, and opened the eyes of millions of citizens to the hidden ways of Wall Street. In each case, stock was offered by J.P. Morgan and Company to the individuals on these lists at cost, or practically at cost. In each case, the offer was made with full and irrefutable knowledge that there was, or would very shortly be, a public market for the stock at a much higher figure. In effect, it was the offer of a gift of very substantial dimensions.

The temptation for such favoritism toward preferred clients has always been there. But in practice, poor corporate governance has come in waves. Unfortunately, in the long view of history, the current crisis appears to be the largest since the tumultuous days of the 1920s and 1930s. Indeed, the long period of growth, stability, and financial restraint that followed the Great Depression and World War II was in many ways a direct outgrowth of those national crises. The economic hardships endured by the Depression generation, reinforced by the new regulatory regime created under Franklin Roosevelt's New Deal, shaped the behavior of a generation of financial leaders and market participants. And to a lesser but still important degree, it also shaped the actions of the generation that followed, who absorbed tales of economic hardship, uncertainty, and struggle from their parents, relatives, and friends.

Such powerful firsthand and secondhand encounters with economic adversity and deep-seated uncertainty are now distant memories. Successive new generations have come to dominate the financial scene. The investors and financial analysts born after the 1950s, 1960s, and 1970s have experienced some business cycles and even a couple of market collapses, but until now they have not seen the integrity of the nation's corporate governance shaken to its foundations. Nor, unfortunately, have the postwar generations learned important lessons from earlier upheavals as part of their business school training.

I say "training" rather than "education" to suggest the narrowness endemic in the curricula of today's undergraduate and graduate business programs. The days when business students were required to take courses in financial history, business history, or even economic history have long passed. Such courses would have instilled in recent business school students some insight into past misbehavior, and why it is so important in financial management to look beyond actions that will have a favorable impact on the immediate future. For too long, business schools have fashioned their course offerings to suit the near-term needs of the financial markets—quantitative risk analysis, model building, spread sheet analysis, and so on. Is it little wonder, then, that too many graduates of such programs have contributed to a culture that favors quick profits and financial buccaneering?

Although it is too early to know for sure, there appear to be some recent efforts to correct this distressing gap in business school education. I certainly hope so. Amid the blizzard of quantitative, technical offerings, our nation's training grounds for its future business leaders surely can make room for courses that offer some deeper perspective on the financial world. Simply put, courses in economic and financial history should be required for all business degrees. I have felt so strongly about this shortcoming for many years that I have personally endowed chairs in these subjects at a number of leading universities. Regrettably, this ignorance of past history seems to be quite pervasive across the entire culture.

The need for effective corporate governance has been heightened over time by the growing separation of ownership and control within leading corporations. This issue is hardly new. One of the most penetrating critiques of the concentration of corporate control appeared back in 1932, when Adolf Berle, a law professor and reformer, and economist Gardiner Means published their landmark book, *The Modern Corporation and Private Property*. As Berle and Means noted vividly:

It has often been said that the owner of a horse is responsible. If the horse lives he must feed it. If the horse dies he must bury it. No such responsibility attaches to a share of stock. The owner is practically powerless through his own efforts to affect the underlying property. The spiritual values that formerly went with ownership have been separated from it. . . . [T]he responsibility and the substance which have been an integral part of ownership in the past are being transferred to a separate group in whose hands lies control.

Indeed, equity investors rarely are involved in the affairs of a corporation in the current environment. Most investment relationships today are fickle. Portfolio performance is measured over very short-term horizons—monthly, quarterly, or at most yearly. Underperformance is penalized very quickly. Today, day trades and portfolio shifts based on the price momentum of the stock—rather than anything having to do with underlying fundamentals—are commonplace. Institutional investors now hold a majority of outstanding stocks, but they remain passive investors for the most part, rarely getting involved in their portfolio companies.

Instead, major institutional shareholders often are brought together in a marriage of convenience with the highest bidder in a corporate takeover. Thus, stockholders are largely temporary holders of certificates that legally meet the definition of equity, but do not embody a true vested interest in the affairs of the company. This detachment is reflected dramatically in the huge increase in annual turnover of the stocks listed on the New York Stock Exchange (NYSE). After holding at around 20 percent on average from the 1960s through the 1980s, turnover of NYSE-listed stocks surged to 75 percent yearly in the 1990s, and now approaches 100 percent.

Given these and related forms of rapid structural transformation, our financial system demands better and more diligent official supervision and regulation. The record shows that regulators have trailed woefully behind technological and institutional change. To be sure, much of what regulators do is remedial, rather than preventive; it comes, by its nature, *in response to* breakdowns and crises. But an imperfect economic democracy such as ours also needs financial supervisors and regulators who can look over the horizon and take reasonable steps to head off crises. And when the system suffers severe problems, as it inevitably will, official supervisors and regulators need to act swiftly and boldly.

Our central bankers at the Federal Reserve, for instance, have simply not been responsive enough to the corrosion that has been infiltrating our financial system in recent years. They appear unwilling to recognize the subtle ways in which financial competition has been diminishing while conflicts of interest have multiplied. In periods of monetary restraint—like the current one—it is common for smaller and medium-sized financial institutions to disappear, leaving only a handful of very large firms. The typical response of central bankers to growing concentration of this sort has been to point out that, when large financial institutions get into trouble, stockholders and lenders are forced to accept losses and the senior management may also be removed. This is hardly a forceful, forward-thinking approach. By the time the central bank intervenes to assist such "too big to fail" institutions, they have often piled up massive excess debt and seriously weakened the entire credit structure.

Not unlike the past, the recent crisis in governance has triggered a series of remedial actions, the most important of which has been the Sarbanes-Oxley legislation promulgated and passed by Congress in 2002. So far, at least, none of the actions taken by Congress and other bodies have restricted financial institutions and markets as severely as the wave of regulations instituted in the 1930s. True, recent legislation put into place tougher standards for auditors, accountants, boards of directors, and securities analysts, as well as for corporate heads and chief financial officers. Much, or all, of this is probably for the good.

But there are some notable blind spots in the new laws for improving corporate governance. One of the chief aims of the new legislation is to significantly improve the transparency and reliability of the information that flows to stockholders and creditors, based on the premise that effective public disclosure will give investors, creditors, and others the information they need to make wise decisions about moving their funds in order to optimize their capital. While that is a worthwhile objective, the practical reality is more problematic. To begin with, few *small* investors possess the knowledge needed to evaluate the complex financial data underlying large financial institutions, especially those with complex holding company structures.

We might also ask: Is the right kind of information flowing out to investors? Naturally, financial information ought to be objective, reliable, consistent with economic realities, and descriptive of the valuation process. But these virtues are complicated by so-called generally accepted accounting principles (GAAP) and by tax accounting. Neither of these filters gives us an accurate picture of an institution's true profits and financial situation—which, after all, is what we really want to know about a financial institution, or indeed any business organization.

Still another key obstacle to sound corporate governance is the shortcomings in accurate marking to market—a weakness that remains woefully unappreciated in the derivatives business. Accurate pricing is the key ingredient for measuring and controlling risk, for calculating profit and loss, and for evaluating performance. Even under normal conditions, this is not a simple and straightforward process, except in certain highly active sectors (such as listed equities and on-the-run U.S. government securities). Rather, for corporate debt obligations, for securities issued by borrowers in emerging markets, and in many segments of the mortgage securities markets, valid pricing is an inexact science. This is most apparent in the pricing of over-the-counter options and of many financial derivatives. In volatile markets, liquidity may disappear suddenly, making the process of marking to market virtually impossible for many of these instruments.

Why is this so? And what are the consequences? To begin with, in rapidly moving markets, the price of the last trade may be completely invalid, particularly for illiquid securities, and certainly for most options.

Second, the price that a dealer is prepared to quote may be little more than an indication of what the security or option is worth, not the price at which the dealer is actually prepared to trade. On that same indications-only basis, another dealer may quote a wildly different price. For the institution trying to mark that position to market, there is no reliable arbiter of the true price. Third, the price quoted may be valid for trading only a very small amount, not the full amount in the investor's portfolio. Fourth, the dealer's assumptions when providing a price for an existing option may be highly questionable, and marking that option position to market cannot be verified by other dealers.

This unsatisfactory state of affairs is hardly new. But the situation has worsened as asset price volatility has surged, because more and more credit obligations have been securitized, and because the securities themselves have become more complex. This is especially true in cases where there is a high degree of what is known technically as "optionality."

Good governance in financial institutions—or in any organization, for that matter—begins at the top, with the integrity and skills of the leaders. Easy as this may sound, it is extremely difficult to attain within large institutions. Whatever a particular leader's skills may be, large financial institutions, typically, are involved in many activities—foreign exchange, investment banking, trading of securities, proprietary position taking, insurance, money management, leasing inventory, and domestic and international markets, among others. Senior management therefore must depend on middle management for a flow of accurate information, but also must rely on the skills of subordinates in modeling risks across a highly diverse range of activities.

Corporate directors face an especially demanding challenge. Each day they must confront the difficult question: How informed should board members be about all the activities and policies of the institutions they serve? In this realm, the line between policy and operations often is blurry. How much should a board member know about transactions with affiliated companies, about the transfer of assets to affiliated entities, or about off-balance-sheet activities? How familiar should a director be with the institution's quantitative risk analysis—its creator, its dynamics, or its underlying historical premise?

My own experience suggests that these and related agency and information quandaries that confront board members can be alleviated in a number of ways. First, new board members should undergo an intensive orientation program. Second, board members need to meet more often—and more intensively—with middle managers, not to discuss operational matters, but rather to reach a common understanding about policy issues. Third, new directors should be required to meet with members of official supervisory agencies such as the Federal Reserve, the Comptroller of the Currency, and the Securities and Exchange Commission, all of whom should explain what these agencies require from the institution and what is required of them as directors. Fourth, new directors should meet with the independent legal counsel who represents them to learn their responsibilities and liabilities from a legal perspective. Fifth, outside auditors should brief new directors on the firm's accounting practices, especially those that fall within contentious gray areas.

I also believe strongly that no matter how much is done now to tighten regulations and the supervision of financial institutions, it will not be enough to counter faulty monetary responses to market developments. While the basic objective of monetary policy is to balance sustainable economic growth with price stability, which most associate with the stability of goods and services, there is, however, another key dimension to be considered: the value of financial assets. Excessive financial asset prices set in motion a series of forces that undermine the very foundation of a stable economy. They stifle incentives to save, breed wasteful business investment, and encourage questionable flows of funds into risky markets at the hand of inexperienced investors. The record shows that, when asset values have fallen suddenly, the Federal Reserve has eased monetary policy to provide greater liquidity in times of stress. But, when asset prices have advanced to speculative heights, escalating financial wealth, the Fed has not responded with alacrity by tightening policy. In the long run, this failure is perhaps more dangerous to the long-term well-being of our economy than any of the private sector financial malpractices that have been in the news in recent years.

In summary, improving governance of financial institutions should be an ongoing imperative and not just come to the fore in the wake of major mishaps and dislocations. Our economy will continue to flourish only as long as institutions learn how to wisely and effectively balance both their entrepreneurial and fiduciary responsibilities.

# 17

# *Transparency and the Fed*

The central mission of the U.S. Federal Reserve is to foster macroeconomic conditions that will encourage long-term economic growth with low inflation. In the post–World War II era, the Fed—in cooperation with the Treasury Department, the Council of Economic Advisers, and other economic policy bodies—has posted an admirable record. (The crippling stagflation of the 1970s is the glaring exception.) And yet, there have been missteps and omissions. Most so-called Fed watchers, when critical of the central bank's actions, point to the timing of this or that increase or decrease in the federal funds rate.

My concern is of a broader magnitude. Simply put, the U.S. Fed has failed to adequately take into account (and adjust its actions accordingly) the massive structural changes that have transformed our economy and our financial markets since the end of the Second World War. These changes, which I have cited throughout this book—securitization, globalization, and the ballooning of public and private debt, among others—have given us a new financial world. The Fed, by and large, continues to operate as if an earlier financial regime still exists. And that, in turn, has contributed significantly to the major economic and financial travails that now plague our system.

I do not mean to suggest that monetary strategy is incapable of responding to structural changes. I have seen it happen. During my early days in the financial markets in the 1950s, the Fed conducted monetary policy by confining open market operations to Treasury bills. Then, for a while in the early 1960s, the Fed shifted to Operation Twist. It sold Treasury bills and bought longer-dated issues in an attempt to defend the stability of the dollar. In those days, market participants eagerly awaited the weekly data on net free or borrowed reserves.

Then, in the 1970s, practical monetarism and, for a short while, strict adherence to monetarism ruled the day. Many readers will recall how every Thursday afternoon markets riveted their attention on the release of the latest money supply numbers. Alas, the concept of the money supply became blurred over time because of many structural changes in financial markets, and by the end of the 1990s the Fed had dropped the money supply as an official target of policy.

Then, as now, monetary policy has tended to lag behind important changes in market structure and investor behavior. Today, the Fed continues to respond belatedly to underlying structural transformation. To be sure, there have been some steps in the right direction. The Basel banking agreements, as well as the Fed's recent efforts at financial market "plumbing"—such as speeding up the documentation of credit derivative transactions—are worthwhile efforts. So, too, are recent official expressions of concern about some of the most entrepreneurial market developments.

But these measures do not go to the heart of the long-term, underlying challenges that now face the U.S. financial system, especially the question of how to enforce discipline. Three possible paths lie ahead. One is to let competitive forces discipline market participants. In this scenario, the managers who perform well will prosper, while those who do not will fail. This is the central tenet of free-market economies. But this approach is compromised by the fact that advanced societies typically do not allow the process to follow through when it comes to very large financial institutions. The failure of behemoth financial conglomerates not only exacts enormous social costs, but also poses systemic risks for markets around the world.

Therefore, market discipline falls unevenly; it falls more heavily on smaller institutions, which in turn motivates them to merge into larger entities protected by the too-big-to-fail umbrella. This dynamic has driven financial concentration, and will continue to do so for years to come. And as financial concentration increases, it will undermine marketability, trading activity, and effective allocation of financial resources. The kinds of financial concentration that sidestep both competition and regulation will continue to weaken the operation of markets over time. In the near term, however, growing financial concentration will continue to spawn heady new financings and trading opportunities.

What about the second path? If competition is not allowed to enforce market discipline, what is the alternative for the monetary authorities? That alternative can only be increased supervision over financial institutions and markets. Even though the financial travails of 2007 and beyond make political conditions more accommodating for tighter oversight, we should not underestimate the difficulties. Most markets participants oppose stiffer regulation, and politicians voice little, if any, support. For their part, central bankers do not possess a clear vision of how to proceed toward more effective financial supervision. Their longstanding, more limited approach seems objectively technical, whereas greater intervention, they fear, would seem intrusive, subjective, even excessive. Witness the very strong criticism of the Sarbanes-Oxley legislation, a measure that surely is far from perfect but came, let us not forget, on the heels of one of the greatest financial market abuses in memory.

What is missing today is a comprehensive framework that pulls together market behavior and economic behavior—a third path. The study

of economics and finance has become highly specialized and compartmentalized within the academic community. This is, of course, another
reflection of the increasing specialization demanded of our complex civi-
lization. Still, I find it regrettable that today's economics and finance pro-
fessions have produced no minds with the analytical reach of Adam Smith
or John Maynard Keynes or Milton Friedman. Perhaps that is too much
to ask for right now.

It may be that the acute economic and financial problems we now
face needed to come first, before new theories and solutions can come
to the forefront. In that sense, problems tend to precede solutions. After
all, Adam Smith and his followers gained prominence following a long
period of mercantilism, which then faced an uncertain future. John
Maynard Keynes came to the fore following the disruptions caused by
World War I, the speculation of the 1920s, and the Great Depression.
And Milton Friedman's teachings gained prominence after years of perplexing stagflation in the 1970s.

In light of this pattern, it seems unlikely that a new economic philosopher will come forth with an integrated economic and financial
approach anytime soon. Today's most influential economists have strong
vested interests in preserving the integrity and reputation of their views.
A lifetime of research and writing is at stake. It is very difficult for any
of us to fundamentally alter our views, especially for those who have
reached a leadership role.

Transparency is a hallmark of modern capitalism, and Federal Reserve
Chairman Ben Bernanke has made transparency a hallmark of his new
regime. Yet among our leading financial institutions, opacity, not financial transparency, has been on the rise. The combination—increasingly
opaque financial markets and increasingly transparent monetary policy—
has created a dangerous brew of financial excesses. Unless both trends
are reversed, financial stability will remain elusive. The explanation for

increasingly opaque financial markets lies chiefly in securitization—the conversion of nonmarketable assets into marketable obligations—which has accelerated dramatically in recent decades.

In theory, securitized markets are supposed to operate on the basis of accurate and readily available prices, the clear assessment of credit quality, and objective analyses of these obligations by rating agencies and by those engaged in trading and underwriting them. Those virtuous mechanisms presumably have been reinforced by a host of new credit instruments, especially financial derivatives that mitigate risk taking. Securitization also has been supported by a dazzling array of new quantitative analytical techniques that are capable, according to practitioners, of defining risk probability down to decimal-point levels.

So what went wrong? In the broadest sense, the structural changes in the financial markets encouraged participants to become short-term oriented.

Financial intermediaries quickly recognized that the process of securitization held the potential for enormous profits—from underwriting, distributing, and trading the newly commodified obligations, as well as from managing them for others. To many, the profit potential seemed virtually unlimited, because it stretched well beyond nonmarketable assets (like a mortgage) and was global in scope. Thus, securitization drove a massive wave of credit creation and helped lift the level of financial-market transactions to record levels.

The new credit entrepreneurship paid off handsomely. For nearly a decade—up to mid-2007—financial profits outpaced the growth of profits in the broader markets.

But the fervor for profits from securitization also ushered in a host of less apparent, and less cheery, institutional shifts. Senior managers at a growing number of leading financial institutions either lost control of risk management or became its captives. In some cases, this happened as managers struggled to understand the dazzling complexity and diversity of the risks assumed by their financial conglomerates. And every institution, of course, felt growing competitive pressure to take on risk in order to maintain market share.

**How Will Mr. Bernanke Measure Up?**

The role of Fed chairman has grown dramatically in the post–World War II years and often overshadows the Treasury secretary. This reflects several key developments. The Fed gained considerable independence from the U.S. Treasury starting in the 1950s when the U.S. government agreed to market rate financing in issuing its new debt. Moreover, the dramatic growth of U.S. financial markets and globalization of markets put the Fed in the center of warding off systemic risks and moderating extreme business cycle fluctuations. Increasingly, it was also recognized that a very flexible fiscal policy that quickly adjusted to economic requirements was unattainable.

It is also easier for the president to replace a Treasury secretary than it is to force a Fed chairman's resignation. A Treasury secretary serves at the pleasure of the president. But a Fed chairman can be removed only by Congress.

Once in office, Fed chairmen usually gain a broad constituency and are viewed as somewhat above the political fray. So most presidents have scrutinized very carefully the economic and monetary philosophy as well as the political leanings of prospective Fed candidates. . . .

Business experience alone does not make for a strong and effective Fed chairman. William Miller—who ran a diversified industrial company when named by Mr. Carter—demonstrated this. Miller was not equipped to grasp the intricacies and fundamental issues of monetary policy. He came to the Fed job when the economy and financial markets were under duress, and left them in even poorer condition.

Mr. Volcker, in contrast, seems almost born and raised to be a central banker. With an education at Princeton University and the London School of Economics, his career moved from economist at the New York Fed and the Chase Bank, to two stints at the U.S. Treasury, to president of the New York Fed, then to the Fed chairmanship.

His dedication to public service is well known. When he became Fed chairman, Mr. Volcker immediately confronted the task of halting a dangerous inflationary spiral. He pursued this relentlessly, though few cheered him on. Fed monetary easing is always more popular than tightening.

Alan Greenspan brought considerable background, including a Ph.D. in economics and prominence as a private sector consultant, as chairman of the Council of Economic Advisers, and as chairman of a government committee that significantly reformed Social Security. During his Fed chairmanship, Mr. Greenspan has navigated the political waters, demonstrating mastery in maintaining unity within the Federal Open Market Committee while maintaining unprecedented public visibility. Time will tell how he will rank among those who preceded him.

And only with the passage of time will the markets feel comfortable with the new chairman. Given our highly entrepreneurial and integrated markets, the new chairman's success will depend largely on an ability to "take away the punch bowl just as the party gets going," in the prophetic words of Bill Martin many years ago.

Excerpt from "The Next Fed Chairman," *Washington Times*, September 6, 2005.

The glamour and profit of risk taking ensured that the risk takers themselves gained more and more power within the structure of financial institutions. With the eclipse of partnerships on Wall Street, investment banks and other financial institutions are now owned by absentee stockholders, the vast majority of whom lack the information and the analytical skills needed to judge the risk portfolios of their institutions. In any case, it is the rare shareholder who will voice displeasure during favorable markets.

Power and decision making increasingly resided in the middle ranks of leading financial institutions. Unlike top managers, who are supposed to take the long view and think strategically, those in the middle ranks—traders, investment bankers, and managers of proprietary activities—compete in areas that are by nature focused on the near term. They are the rainmakers. They and their institutions thrive on profits from securitized markets and on ever-expanding asset markets. They are biased to pursue ever greater levels of risk.

Incentive systems within financial institutions offer few restraints. It is possible, though rare, for top managers to be removed from office. But even then, judging by recent events, compensation packages for the deposed are more than generous. Middle managers are sometimes dismissed, but they too typically received generous termination payments as part of their contractual arrangements. Such arrangements are net losses for employers, for there are no claw-back provisions to recoup any of the losses incurred by the former managers.

As financial markets have become opaque and risk-laden, the Federal Reserve has touted its own growing transparency. Yet the central bank has made no real effort to compel financial institutions to follow suit. When the Fed failed to put into place new disclosure requirements or otherwise penetrate market opacity, market participants took note and devised new ways to camouflage risk and create additional excessive credit.

Some of the structured investment vehicles (SIVs) that contributed to the recent hemorrhaging of the money market were an off-balance-sheet activity of bank holding companies—and therefore subject to Federal Reserve supervision. But the Fed seemed satisfied to allow them, as long as it determined that the value-at-risk procedure employed by these holding companies fell within generally accepted parameters.

Rather than focus on the threat posed by the lack of transparency, the Fed has focused on mechanical deficiencies in the market. For instance, regulators tried to ensure that the huge volume of trades would be cleared quickly and with correct documentation. This is worthwhile, but by itself cannot forestall credit abuses. By failing to acknowledge and attack risks posed by opaque financial practices, the Fed encouraged them.

Ironically, the Fed's own transparency—as demonstrated by the new tenor of the central bank's open market pronouncements in recent years—has tended to foster rather than dampen financial excesses. Perhaps nothing better illustrates the Fed's lack of preemptive restraint than what has become known in the investment community as the Greenspan put. Briefly stated, this is the now-prevailing view that monetary authorities do not know when a full-blown credit bubble is upon us, but they do know what to do once a bubble bursts. I have long argued this approach condones excessive credit growth. Massive infusion of new funds following a major market collapse can provide temporary relief, but it does not repair the long-term political, social, and economic damage caused by the meltdown. How can this monetary approach not reduce market discipline before the collapse, or incite a quick return to speculative activities after the Fed rescue?

Consider another example of the Fed's transparency policy that is likely to backfire. In November 2007, the Fed announced that it would increase the "frequency and content" of its economic projections released to the public. Rather than twice a year, the Fed planned to announce them quarterly; and it would extend the forecast horizon to three years from two.

At first blush, these might seem like moves in a positive direction. But will they actually diminish market opacity or restrain market activity within prudent bounds? This is highly unlikely. That is the case, at least, for the Fed's first more detailed economic pronouncement, which predicted moderate economic growth for the next three years, inflation to remain within acceptable bounds, and high resource utilization, as measured by the unemployment rate. In contrast, if the Fed were to project a significant escalation in the inflation rate or a sharp cyclical turn to a business recession, financial markets would recoil, and the central bank would be blamed for damaging the economy. What would be more helpful is what is currently missing from the Fed's current repertoire: the central bank's assessment of financial developments for the next three years, and the specific interest rate range needed if the Fed is to achieve its economic targets.

At the heart of the Federal Reserve's diminished influence as a positive economic influence is its ambivalent core philosophy. During his long tenure as Fed chairman, Alan Greenspan ostensibly was an economic libertarian. This means not only that the market knows best, but that the market should decide winners and losers. I say "ostensibly" because, like Mr. Greenspan and the central bank that continues in the shadow of his legacy, most Americans applaud competition while being uncomfortable with certain kinds of personal and institutional failure. There is no better example than our attitudes about the failure of large financial institutions.

With huge liabilities resting on a thin capital base, they are vulnerable giants. Yet they are the custodians of the public's temporary funds, savings, and investments. They cannot be allowed to fail. The costs—financially and economically, socially and politically, domestically and internationally—are unacceptable. So many economic libertarians such as Alan Greenspan live uncomfortably with the doctrine of "too big to fail." Nevertheless, one cannot be a true advocate of the philosophy by adhering to it when monetary ease is the order of the day and abandoning it when market discipline punishes those who have committed financial excesses.

Even out of office, Mr. Greenspan continues to want it both ways. His best-selling memoir reasserts his laissez-faire philosophy, but in a recent pronouncement he advocated giving funds directly to needy subprime mortgage borrowers to permit them to meet their contractual mortgage obligations. This would have three consequences. It would alleviate the immediate pain of the borrowers (who should not have been allowed to borrow in the first place). It would keep the facade of the financial system in place without disciplining excessive lending practices. And it would socialize the cost of the problem by raising the government's budget deficit.

Today, a shrinking number of huge, integrated financial conglomerates dominate markets. They offer a full range of financial services— commercial banking, investment banking, insurance, credit cards, asset management, mutual funds, pension funds, and so on. But annual reports, 10-K reports, and other currently required reporting tools give us little idea of the true extent of their risk-taking activities. A rough calculation of the proportion of risk exposure to tangible financial assets within these institutions suggests a ratio of dozens of dollars at risk for each one in hand.

# PART VI
# PROSPECTS

# 18

# *Prospects for*
# *Interest Rates*

The current credit crisis has left a deeper imprint on the American money and capital markets than any other financial crisis since the end of World War II. Some markets, including commercial paper and money market funds, clogged up and required Federal Reserve support. The Fed established a Commercial Paper Funding Facility (CPFF). The subprime mortgage market closed down for new borrowers, with the secondary markets seeing only sparse trading at sharply lower prices. Many large financial institutions saw their creditworthiness come under close scrutiny as their share prices plummeted. The stocks of Citigroup and Bank of America, the two largest U.S. banks, have traded below $5 a share, unimaginable a matter of months ago.

Along with its commercial paper market rescue operations, the Federal Reserve increased its lending program to commercial banks and purchased billions of dollars of their assets and currency swaps. This was followed by the Term Asset-Backed Securities Loan Facility (TALF), a Federal Reserve program designed to improve the markets for securities backed by student loans, credit card receivables, auto loans, and small business loans. All of these activities increased the Fed's own balance sheet footings from $869 billion at the end of 2007 to a peak of $2.1 trillion at the end of 2008.

Lost amid the headlines about failing investment banks, the ailing mortgage market, and federal stimulus packages is a watershed in the history of interest rates—the end of a half-century-long secular swing. In fact, we now stand at the tail end of the greatest secular swing in interest rates in U.S. history. Secular swings are long-term movements that span years or decades and are punctuated by shorter cyclical movements. The pattern observed in Exhibit 18.1—which shows yields on the U.S. Treasury's 30-year long bond over the past six decades—is unmistakable. The upward move began in 1946, when long bonds were yielding 2.16 percent, and ended in October 1981, when they peaked at 15.25 percent. Thereafter, yields on 30-year bonds fell irregularly to a low of 2.69 percent in early 2009, which probably marks the end of this extended wave.

The magnitude of this long up-and-down yield movement dwarfs by a very wide margin all four previous secular swings in American financial history. The cumulative change in the postwar trough-to-peak-to-trough swings was 25.3 percentage points. In the prior four secular swings, the largest change was just 5.6 percentage points, and

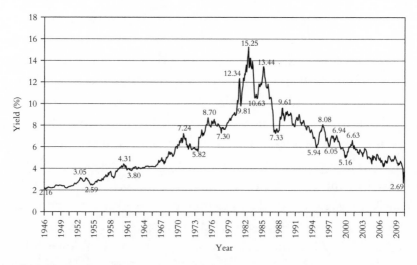

**Exhibit 18.1**    Yield on Long-Term U.S. Government Bonds, 1946–2009

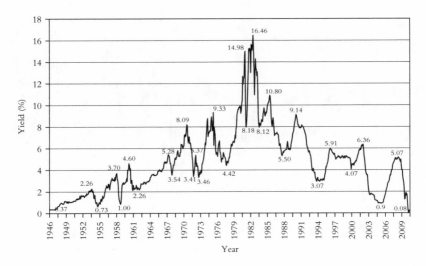

**Exhibit 18.2** Yields on Three-Month Treasury Bills, 1946–2009

that occurred in the much shorter period from 1810 to 1824. Indeed, the current secular swing is much longer than any previous wave.

The secular swings in three-month U.S. Treasury bill yields mirror the contours of the long U.S. bond yield wave, yet with even more extreme dimensions (see Exhibit 18.2). Three-month Treasuries started at 37 basis points in 1946, reached 16.46 percent at their extreme peak in 1980, and fell to nearly zero early this year. The very low bill yields early this year match their behavior during the Great Depression, reflecting the frantic search by investors for liquidity and safety.

Another way of looking at these interest rate movements is to examine the difference—known as the yield curve—between the yields on long U.S. government bonds and three-month U.S. Treasury bills. When the yield curve is positive, long yields exceed short-term rates. When it is negative, short-term interest rates exceed the yield on long-term bonds. As shown in Exhibit 18.3, there have been many extremes in this yield differential since 1946. The extreme positive differential has been greater than 3 percentage points six times. Only once were negative spreads that wide; five of them were less than 1 percentage point.

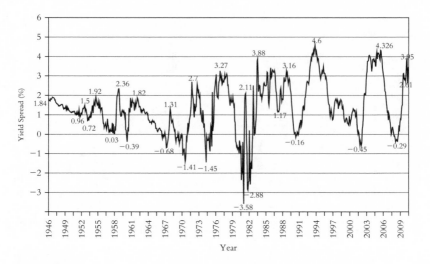

**Exhibit 18.3**   30-Year/Three-Month Treasury Yield Spread, 1946–2009

Yield curve trends can provide clues about the future direction of long government bond yields. First, when the yield curve moves from flat to extremely positive (with long yields going above short), long yields fall in conjunction with a more sizable drop in short rates. This happened during the past few years. Second, the swing from an extremely positive to a flat yield curve often is quite perilous in the long bond market. Third, the most dangerous period of all for investors in long bonds is when the yield curve moves from flat to extremely negative, with short rates shooting up above long rates.

With these caveats in mind, what are the prospects for the yields on U.S. government securities? To begin with, it is very likely the long secular decline in interest rates is over. Short-term rates will linger around their current very low levels until the Federal Reserve abandons its quantitative easing approach. At a minimum, this will last until the mortgage sector bottoms out or, more likely, begins to improve. The Federal Reserve also will await evidence that the key inflationary indicators are beginning to creep up again along with the employment rate. The soonest the Fed will begin to shift away from its current posture—and even then, gradually—probably is sometime in 2010.

In contrast, long U.S. government bond yields already have moved up from the extreme secular low they reached at the start of 2009. More irregular upward movements are likely in the months to come. The huge financing needs of the U.S. Treasury will hold back a significant rally while frequently pushing long U.S. bond yields somewhat higher. The Federal Reserve will help prevent significant setbacks in this market through its purchases of longer-dated U.S. government bonds. The eventual return of private-sector credit demands combined with high U.S. government issuance (noted earlier) will drive up long-term interest rates. In the meantime, the government yield curve will grow steeper, propelled by long U.S. government bond yields, which probably will increase into the range of 5½ to 6 percent in 2010.

Interest rates in the corporate bond market will trace a different pattern. Long corporate bond yields will continue to be influenced by the capacity of corporations to maintain their earning power. As the business recession drags on for most, if not all, of 2009, constraints on corporate pricing power will cause further deterioration in corporate credit quality. The universe of below-investment-grade corporate bonds that has grown steadily in the past few decades will expand rapidly in the months to come. A plethora of corporate failures also will unsettle the bond market. As a result, the current wide differential in yields between U.S. government and corporate bonds will narrow only slightly (see Exhibit 18.4).

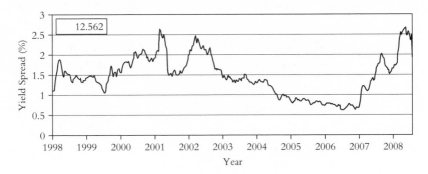

**Exhibit 18.4**   Yield Differentials between Corporate Bonds and 10-Year U.S. Government Bonds

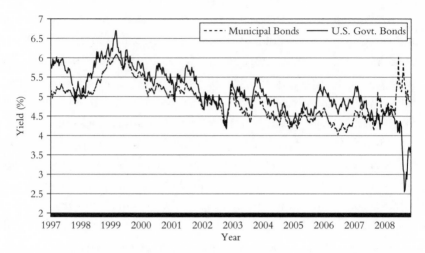

**Exhibit 18.5**    Yields on 20-Year Municipal Government Bonds and 30-Year
U.S. Government Bonds

The municipal bond target will also be confronted with credit
problems. The economic recession is taking a heavy toll on state and
local government revenues. Such budget pressures will lead to significant expenditure slowdowns, with some of the slack taken up by federal
government assistance. Credit quality is likely to deteriorate. And, acting
belatedly, rating agencies will lower credit ratings. As a result, the attractive yield differential between long U.S. governments and municipals
will continue to favor municipal obligations until the next economic
recovery is well established (see Exhibit 18.5). In the history of American
interest rates, that yield differential has been quite uncommon.

In the longer term, the path of interest rates will largely depend
on the lessons learned from the current financial debacle. Like those
who endured the Great Depression and carried its scars into the years
that followed, most Americans today will not quickly forget the devastation caused by the latest crisis. It is driving down expectations and

dampening aggressive lending and investing practices. For its part, the U.S. government needs to put in place policies that will induce financial institutions to balance their entrepreneurial drive with their fiduciary responsibilities. And if that happens, future interest rate swings should be more moderate than the gyrations that have marked most decades in the postwar period.

# 19

# *The Financial Consequences of the Credit Crisis*

The financial crisis of 2007 will reshape the financial world for years to come. Some of the key consequences—such as the revival of household savings, the eclipse of risk modeling, and the persistence of the U.S. dollar as the leading reserve currency—are welcomed. But others, most notably the explosion of public debt and the acceleration of financial concentration, portend trouble.

The dimensions of the current credit crisis are in many ways close to those of the Great Depression of the 1930s. Although the economy has not reached the depths of the Depression, neither the economic crisis nor the financial crisis has run its course as this book goes to press. And on the financial side, there are some striking parallels between the two upheavals. At the onset of the Great Depression, stock prices plummeted 83 percent from their peak in late 1929 to their trough in the summer of 1932. In the current crisis, the Dow fell 55 percent, from 14,198 in October 2007 to 6,469 in March 2009.

In the credit markets, movements have been even more ominous than in the equities markets. Back in the late 1920s, the aggregate asset size of the major financial institutions—which then consisted of commercial banks, thrift deposit institutions, and private life insurance companies—more or less matched the U.S. gross national product (GNP). Today, total assets held by the much wider array of financial institutions are several multiples of GNP. The current size of the financial derivatives market, with its web of international linkages, dwarfs GNP. At the same time, many of our major financial institutions are nearly inoperative, with the shares of some of the very largest trading more than 90 percent below their highs, in some cases in single digits.

In spite of the differences in scale and scope between the two eras, there are some underlying commonalities. In his 1970 book *America's Greatest Depression, 1929–1941*, Lester V. Chandler observed that "financial institutions were in distress because their owners were dishonest, or at the very least had betrayed their trust in managing other people's money. They loaded up with domestic loans and securities that would have proved unsound even if prosperous conditions had continued, and that certainly could not weather even a mild depression." The passage could have been written today.

To cope with the calamity, the federal government injected massive amounts of capital into the financial system, mainly into the largest institutions. The government also took over two huge federally sponsored mortgage institutions, Fannie Mae and Freddie Mac. The nation's fifth largest investment bank, Bear Stearns, buckling under mounting liquidity pressures, was forced to sell at a distressed price to JPMorgan Chase. Lehman Brothers, the fourth largest investment bank, failed. All the other remaining large, independent investment banks rushed to organize commercial banking entities in order to be put under the Federal Reserve umbrella.

In view of the severity of the current financial crisis, profound consequences for the financial markets are likely for years to come. Although there have been more than a dozen crises since the end of World War II, the aftermath of each of those episodes was transitory—markets rebounded, lending and investing sped up again, and risk taking moved up several notches. Given the depth and broad dimensions of the current crisis, it will usher in significant and lasting structural, behavioral, and regulatory changes. Already it has begun to produce consequences that are reshaping the growth of debt, the structure of financial institutions, the course of interest rates (the subject of the previous chapter), the supervision of financial institutions, the nature of portfolio management, and the role of the U.S. dollar in the foreign exchange markets.

The current crisis has brought an end to a decades-long period of private sector debt growth. The institutions that facilitated rapid debt growth in recent decades are now virtually disabled, their borrowers overloaded. While this debt boom was unfolding, it created euphoria in financial markets and unsustainable economic growth.

The magnitude of debt creation in recent years was unprecedented. Since 2000, the growth of nonfinancial debt has outpaced the growth of nominal gross domestic product (GDP) by nearly $8 trillion—more than double the $3.5 billion gap of the 1990s, which already was excessive (see Exhibit 13.1).

In the private sector, the slowdown has already begun. Household debt, which grew at an annual average of 10.7 percent from 2001 through 2006, increased by 6.8 percent in 2007; but it grew at an annual average of only 1.9 percent in the first half of 2008, and actually contracted by 0.8 percent in the second half of that year. And this slowdown is unlikely to reverse anytime soon, in part because it is being compounded by troubling trends in unemployment, which will continue to rise well into 2010, and personal income, which at best will increase much less than the long-term trend for some time to come.

The growth of household debt also is being constrained by a dramatic slowdown in securitization, which contributed so much to the increase in household borrowing and a consequent overload of household debt. As a practical matter, financial institutions now simply lack the capacity to hold a huge volume of securitized obligations in temporary inventory. This is because the leverage capacity of lenders is shrinking, thereby limiting the loan facilities needed to carry the same volume of securitized obligations.

At the same time, securitization will come under closer scrutiny. Much of its success had depended on accurate mark-to-market pricing of involved assets traded on secondary markets, many of which became very problematic. Current marking-to-market practices are not uniform and therefore have injected risk and uncertainty into the market. Such practices will be discontinued—another serious constraint on future debt creation.

Like private debt, business debt growth will slow appreciably, a process already under way. Business debt increased annually nearly 11 percent during the three years that ended in 2007. In the second half of 2008, it slowed to an annual rate of 3 percent. The constraints on corporate borrowing include a weak profit picture, a sharp reduction in capital spending, and corporate debt overload. The latter will become increasingly visible in the next 12 months as an unhealthy trend in the corporate credit structure becomes apparent: Credit rating agencies are going to lower corporate debt ratings at an accelerating pace. This troubling trend—the weakening credit structure of businesses—was masked during the previous business cycle by robust corporate profits. During the run-up, however, businesses increased their leverage by issuing proportionally more debt while retiring outstanding equity. At the close of 2004, the market value of nonfinancial corporate equity stood at $12.1 trillion, compared with total corporate debt of $5.2 trillion. By the end of 2008, equity value was down to $9.6 trillion while debt had risen to $7.1 trillion. As a result, corporate credit ratings continued to perform poorly. Unfortunately, falling credit ratings are likely to outnumber rising ones in the next few years.

While household and business debt creation decelerate, U.S. government debt will explode. The federal stimulus program of tax reduction and new spending initiatives is likely to increase the national debt by $3 trillion or $4 trillion in the next few years—perhaps even more, depending on the scale of funds needed to bail out U.S. financial institutions. For a while, the federal government will find itself competing for funds against waning private-sector demands (as noted earlier). There is a silver lining: The combination of shrinking private sector demands and expanding federal demands will improve the credit quality of many portfolios. This is especially beneficial for many overleveraged financial institutions. They will be able to engage in carry trades—investing in longer-dated U.S. government securities with shorter-dated borrowings.

Although this investment technique poses no credit risk, it does pose a money rate risk. When interest rates rise, the carry trades incur losses. So far, the Federal Reserve has encouraged carry trades. It announced that it is prepared to go into the market and buy outright longer-dated U.S. government bonds, presumably to stabilize yields and to limit the negative impact that higher-yielding government bonds would have on other sectors of the bond market, especially mortgages. In the past, the Federal Reserve occasionally intervened in the markets to achieve certain interest rate objectives with rather mixed results. For example, when the U.S. dollar was under attack in the early 1960s, the Federal Reserve pursued an approach called Operation Twist. To support the dollar, it sold Treasury bills, thereby encouraging money rates to stay or rise above current levels; and the Fed bought longer-dated issues to hold or reduce long-term yields in order to maintain the flow of long-term funds to the private sector.

In the current crisis, the markets will carefully monitor the yield trend of the 10-year U.S Treasury obligations. This is because yields in this sector provide benchmarks for yields on mortgages. When the Federal Reserve comes in to buy these issues, the yield at the time of Fed intervention will be viewed as the upper end of the yield range that is acceptable to the Fed. If the central bank fails to defend that upper yield level, the result will be additional dramatic upward lurches in yields. This poses a dilemma for the Federal Reserve, which will want to disengage when the credit crisis is over and markets are better able to function on the basis of supply-and-demand considerations. But if the Fed acts prematurely, it may contribute to an anemic economic recovery. If it acts belatedly, its actions may spur undue speculation and excessive credit growth.

It is also quite likely that in spite of the best intentions and efforts by government officials, the near nationalization of residential housing through the federal takeover of Fannie Mae and Freddie Mac will take years to reverse, assuming it ever happens. This is because, for homeowners, the cost of securing mortgage finance directly from the U.S. government is much lower than the cost of financing through private institutions, as well as the cost that prevailed while Fannie and Freddie were still functioning as government-sponsored agencies. Therefore, shifting residential housing finance back to more expensive private-sector institutions will require considerable political will. Even if Fannie and Freddie are restricted to issuing and securitizing mortgages and required to sell off securitized assets to the private sector, still political opposition is likely.

In the broadest sense, several developments are worth noting. Americans will begin to save again. The personal savings rate (as a percentage of disposable personal income) has been tepid for years, and actually fell below zero in 2006. Since then it has remained for the most part at the low end of positive, perplexing many economists and policy makers. The government has provided some incentives, such as deferred profit-sharing plans and allowing taxpayers to deposit their refunds into individual retirement accounts (IRAs). But in spite of these well-intended programs, the net saving rate for households has not improved; savers simply reallocated where they put their money. I have believed for many years that the erosion of personal savings is chiefly the result of massive debt creation. The ready access to borrowing has blurred the difference between a liability and an asset. Easy access to credit through credit cards, lines of credit, equity loans on houses, reverse mortgages, and other easy channels has simultaneously discouraged households from saving while encouraged a borrowing binge that heaped up enormous debt-service burdens.

This relaxation of American attitudes about savings is quite visible in the debt and savings data in the past half century. From 1960 to 1990, the average growth rate of nonfinancial debt exceeded that of nominal GDP by 1.5 times, while the savings rate averaged 9 percent per year. From 1991 to 2000, debt growth exceeded GDP growth by 1.8 times, while the savings rate averaged 4.7 percent. Since 2001, debt has grown twice as fast as GDP, while the savings rate has averaged a mere 1.4 percent. The lesson is clear: If the savings rate is to return to healthy levels, we must put an end to the reckless creation of debt.

In the wake of the current crisis, portfolio managers will change some of their longstanding methods. One is risk modeling, popular among portfolio managers for quite some time but about to fall out of fashion. Because techniques used to model risk in financial institutions are backward-looking (in the sense that they reset on historical dates), they are essentially useless in times of fundamental structural change such as the markets are undergoing now. Elaborate modeling formulas for options and other complex financial derivatives that are useful for dynamic hedging under normal circumstances are of little use when transactions cannot be made without huge price concessions. Stated differently, most models rest on assumptions about normal, rational financial behavior, but lose their predictive power during times of financial euphoria or panic. Consequently, the magnitude of the current crisis calls into question whether, even after markets stabilize, sophisticated risk modeling can regain its former status.

International portfolio diversification will lose popularity as well. This investment strategy, long heralded by portfolio practitioners and leading academicians, has failed to weather the test of the current credit crisis. In the 2008 sell-off, many non-U.S. stock indexes fell more than U.S. equities, a trend especially pronounced in very popular developing countries, where there was a growing belief among investors that their economies would perform largely independently of the industrialized world. But this expectation of decoupling has proven to be illusory.

The fact is, developing nations depend heavily on the developed world to consume their products and services and to finance their business activities. They still lack deep financial markets and strong legal structures to support their political systems—weaknesses that are quickly exposed by increasingly globalized financial markets. When liquidity is ample and credit readily available, developing economies thrive; but when global credit comes under pressure, they suffer even more than their more developed counterparts. This is why the strategy of international portfolio diversification needs to be rethought and improved for it to remain an abiding principle of asset allocation.

During and after the current crisis, financial concentration will gain even greater momentum and influence unless it is restrained by legislation. If not, the concentration of markets and assets into the hands of a smaller and smaller number of enormous diversified financial giants will prove to be the most profound long-term consequence of the current financial crisis. Building on a trend that already had reached epic proportions, in recent months leading independent investment banks and giant deposit institutions have been taken over by large financial conglomerates that are in turn controlled by commercial banking entities. Within the next year, many smaller and medium-sized financial institutions also will lose their independent identities. Today, more than half of all nonfinancial debt is held by the top 15 institutions. These were the very firms that played a central role in creating debt on an unprecedented scale through a process of massive securitization via complex new credit instruments.

They also pushed for legal structures that made many aspects of the financial markets opaque.

In the years ahead, the influence of these financial conglomerates will be overwhelming. Most important, they will limit any chance for the United States to move toward greater economic democracy. They are and will continue to be infused with conflicts of interest because of their multiple roles in securities underwriting, in lending and investing, in the making of secondary markets, and in the management of other people's money. And because there will be few market participants of importance, the price volatility of financial assets likely will remain high. Through their global reach, these sprawling firms will transmit financial contagion even more quickly than it spread in the current credit crisis. When the current crisis abates, the pricing power of these huge financial conglomerates will grow significantly, at the expense of borrowers and investors.

Despite the travails in the U.S. economy and financial markets, the U.S. dollar will remain the key reserve currency. To be sure, there are recurring concerns: that large foreign holders will aggressively push to diversify; that investment opportunities will be more attractive elsewhere; and that U.S. policy will not effectively cope with rising inflation that simulative fiscal and monetary policies might spark. But unless the world rushes to plow funds into hard assets on a massive scale, no real alternative to the U.S. dollar will emerge for some time to come. Even though the dollar will come under pressure periodically, it will remain the key currency.

The dollar's chief rival, the euro, faces serious challenges. The immediate one is a business recession—sharply falling business profits combined with the constraints that hinder overleveraged financial institutions. The United States confronts many of the same obstacles, but, unlike Europe, it is unified politically. The euro functions as a single currency without effective controls on the ability of individual governments to control debt. No formal procedure is in place to aid member govern-ments when they are experiencing economic difficulties. Cross-border labor mobility has not been of sufficient scale to offset economic differ-ences among the member countries. More than that, the European Cen-tral Bank has not succeeded in fashioning policies that equitably serve the needs of the diverse nations under its mandate. Already, the credit ratings of the peripheral members of the euro zone are questionable, and their borrowing costs are rising relative to Germany. Will some of these countries try to abandon the euro? Edward Chancellor recently pointed to another possibility: "Germany might be forced to reluctantly make huge fiscal transfers to euro zone countries with large current account deficits, such as Spain."

Another drawback for the euro is growing Russian belligerence. By itself, this casts a shadow broad enough to discourage massive flows out of the dollar.

Two other currencies occasionally are suggested as alternatives to the U.S. dollar. One is the Japanese yen. To a large extent, this reflects the periodic strength of this currency. But Japan lacks the financial insti-tutional framework to support the yen as a reserve currency, and the country's economy has slipped into another recession. China's currency, the renminbi, also is mentioned as a future U.S. dollar alternative. Even if this ever were to happen, it will be a long way off. Among other things, China does not possess a strong legal system. It also lacks well-developed money and capital market institutions, a freely traded currency, and a sufficient number of private-sector business and financial organizations for the renminbi to serve as a reserve currency.

The current turmoil in financial markets and its aftermath make cer-tain that the stakes associated with regulatory reform are very high. While the need to reform financial oversight is widely acknowledged, what is less well understood is the extraordinary balancing act U.S. lawmakers must achieve. On the one hand, the new regulatory regime needs to be comprehensive enough to take into account major structural changes that have unfolded in recent decades. On the other hand, it must assure reasonable credit growth and competitive credit markets. Each new measure will impinge on embedded interests, making the whole enterprise—essential as it is to our nation's economic health—a major political contest.

Given the breadth and depth of the current financial crisis, many market participants have been called to account. But I am convinced that the misbehavior of some would have been much rarer—and far less damaging to our economy—if the Federal Reserve and, to a lesser extent, other supervisory authorities had measured up to their responsibilities.

More than any other entity, the Federal Reserve is the guardian of our financial system. The role of a financial guardian is somewhat akin to that of a parent. A parent should not be a friend to his or her child but should rather hold the child accountable to a set of clear, consistent, and fair behavioral standards. In similar fashion, the official guardian of our financial system must hold financial institutions to a code of conduct, and never should be viewed as a friend or a hero of Wall Street or other interest groups. By the very nature of their responsibility, the leaders of the Fed should not become folk heroes. Indeed, the "rules of the game" is a key concept in economics, for without such rules market economies cannot function. Recently, Albert Wojnilower drew a memorable parallel between financial rules and the rules that govern sports. "All organized sports depend on rules and boundaries—and referees. Even children are coached to evade the rules when the referee is not looking. . . . But without referees, and police [who] watch the referees, there would be no game. The same is true for financial markets."

Seen in this way, much of the recent extreme financial behavior is rooted in faulty monetary policies. Poor policies encourage excessive risk

taking. Too often in recent decades, the Federal Reserve followed policies that failed to recognize, in a timely fashion, behavioral and structural
changes in the marketplace. At the same time, the Fed has espoused a
laissez-faire economic ideology while failing to follow it consistently.
Both of these shortcomings played a central role in steering the U.S.
economy onto an unsustainable path. Accordingly, to emerge from the
current muddle and chart a sounder course, we need to fundamentally
reconsider the role of the Federal Reserve and, more broadly, the supervision of our financial institutions.

In the current crisis, the Fed's performance can be judged through
the lens of two key questions. What did monetary policy makers
do to prevent, or at least mitigate, the crisis? And what actions did
the central bankers undertake once they recognized the enormity of the
problem?

I hardly need to demonstrate here that the Fed failed to recognize
promptly the dimensions of the credit crisis; this already has been well
documented. Just a few months before the credit problems were in full
bloom, senior Fed officials stated that the subprime mortgage problem
was well contained. Right up to the brink of the crisis, monetary officials continued to profess the view that our financial institutions were
strong. Only when the credit problem became abundantly clear did the
Fed begin to move gradually to contain it.

Fortunately, after this belated start, the central bank began to act with
full force and considerable ingenuity. It put forth a series of countermea-
sures, including the Term Auction Facility (TAF), an emergency lending
authority to provide primary dealers access to central bank credit; the
Term Securities Lending Facility, which lends Treasury securities to dealers; programs that backstop money market funds; a Commercial Paper
Funding Facility (CPFF); the Term Asset-Backed Securities Loan Facility (TALF); and the purchase of high-quality assets, including private
credit obligations. The Fed also facilitated the purchase of Bear Stearns
by JPMorgan Chase and prevented the default of American International Group (AIG). I mention all these Fed measures to give full credit

to the Fed's resourcefulness and innovativeness in working to revive the credit market. For this, the Fed deserves to be commended. Even so, these actions came after the crisis had gained considerable momentum.

The Fed has been hobbled by at least two major shortcomings. One has been its failure to recognize the significance for monetary policy of structural changes in the financial markets, changes that surfaced quite early in the post–World War II era. In 1962, in the first in a series of deregulatory measures, the Fed raised the Regulation Q ceiling on the interest rate paid on time and savings deposits. While I do not criticize this action, it seemed to me at the time that the Fed failed to incorporate this liberalization into its policy formulations. Abandoning Regulation Q enabled banks to become intermediaries, in the sense that they no longer had to bear the money rate risk. As long as these institutions could maintain a favorable spread between the cost of liabilities and the return on their assets, it no longer mattered to bankers how high interest rates were pushed by the monetary authorities. The combination of the freedom to bid for funds in the open market and the advent of floating-rate financing became a powerful force for the creation of new credit. This new dynamic had serious long-range consequences. Because the relationship between the availability of funds and the demanders of credit had changed, interest rates now had to be driven up to extraordinary heights for the central bank to achieve a restraining effect, or credit quality had to deteriorate rapidly to cause market alarm.

We now have learned the hard way that financial deregulation still facilitates the creation of debt because it spurs competition and reinforces the drive for new markets and enlarged market standing. Monetary policy makers neither anticipated these realities nor incorporated them into their policy calculations.

The Federal Reserve also failed to grasp early (or with sufficient clarity later on) the significance of financial innovations that, by their very nature, facilitate the creation of new credit—innovations that could not have been financed at all using earlier techniques. Perhaps the most far-reaching of these innovations was the securitization of nonmarketable obligations. This tended to create the illusion that credit risk could be reduced if the instruments became marketable. Quite a few holders of securitized obligations believed they had the foresight to sell before markets adjusted to a decrease in creditworthiness. Moreover, elaborate new techniques employed in securitization (such as credit guarantees and insurance) blurred credit risks and—from my perspective many years ago—raised the vexing question, "Who is the real guardian of credit?" Instead of addressing these issues, the Federal Reserve actually was highly supportive of securitization. Alan Greenspan, when he was Fed chairman, stated that securitization was very beneficial because it helped spread risk over a broader spectrum of the financial markets.

One of the Federal Reserve's biggest blind spots when it comes to structural changes has been its failure to recognize the problems that huge financial conglomerates would pose for financial stability—including their key role in the current debt overload. The Fed allowed the Glass-Steagall Act to succumb without much fanfare and without appreciating the negative consequences of its demise. Within two decades or so, financial conglomerates—or, as some like to call them, large integrated financial institutions—have come to utterly dominate financial markets and financial behavior. The 10 largest U.S. financial institutions now hold more than 50 percent of U.S. financial assets, up from only 10 percent in 1990. The 20 largest institutions hold now more than 70 percent, compared with 12 percent at the start of 1990. In fact, the latest credit crisis increased financial concentration by leaps and bounds.

Official policy makers actually encouraged huge financial institutions to merge in order to avoid insolvency and market disruptions. But monetary policy makers failed to recognize that these financial behemoths are honeycombed with conflicts of interest that interfere with effective credit allocation. Instead of cultivating transparency about their myriad activities, financial conglomerates have become more and more opaque, especially about their massive off-balance-sheet activities. The Fed failed to rein in the problem, even when off-balance-sheet entities were created by subsidiaries of bank holding companies over which the Fed has direct oversight. The structured investment vehicles (SIVs) that financed longer-dated mortgages by issuing commercial paper are a now-infamous example.

Nor did the Fed recognize the crucial role that the large financial conglomerates have played in changing the public's perception of liquidity. Traditionally, liquidity was an asset-based concept. But in recent decades this shifted to the liability side, as liquidity came to be virtually synonymous with very easy access to borrowing. That would not have happened without the massive marketing efforts of large institutions, which of course have issued billions of credit cards and aggressively promoted seamless ways to enlarge mortgage debt. The same leading firms also created a panoply of debt obligations designed to finance corporate mergers and takeovers. All of this contributed to the loosening of credit standards.

My second major concern about the conduct of monetary policy is the Fed's prevailing philosophy of economic libertarianism. At the heart of this economic dogma, as it pertains to monetary policy, is the belief that markets know best and that those who compete well will prosper while those who do not will fail.

How did this affect the Fed's actions and behavior? First, it explains to a large extent why the Fed did not strongly oppose the removal of the Glass-Steagall Act, the demise of which in turn contributed to a massive consolidation of the financial system.

Second, it also helps explain why the Fed failed to recognize that abandoning Glass-Steagall created more institutions that would be considered too big to fail. The Fed never admitted that large institutions were too big to fail until the current crisis took hold.

Third, it diminished the supervisory role of the Fed, especially its direct responsibility to regulate bank holding companies. To be sure, the Fed's supervisory responsibilities never have been very visible in the monetary policy decision-making process. But its tilt toward an economic libertarian approach pushed supervision a notch down just at a time when financial market complexity was on the rise.

Fourth, as hands-on supervision slackened, quantitative risk modeling became increasingly acceptable. This approach, especially quantitative modeling to assess the safety of a financial institution, was—considering the complexity of markets and the vast structural changes in the markets—far from adequate. But it worked hand in glove with a philosophy that markets know best.

Fifth, adherence to economic libertarianism inhibited the Fed from using the bully pulpit or moral suasion to constrain market excesses. Alan Greenspan spoke about irrational exuberance only as a theoretical concept, not as a warning to the market to curb excessive behavior. It is difficult to believe that recourse to moral suasion by a Fed chairman would be ineffective. Such public pronouncements about financial excesses are hard to ignore. They reach not only major market participants but the broad public as well.

Sixth, the Fed's increasingly libertarian philosophy also underpinned its view that it could not know how to recognize a credit bubble, but it knew what to do once a credit bubble burst. This approach, which became known in the markets as the Greenspan put, offered considerable solace to risk takers. But it is a philosophy plagued with fallacies. Credit bubbles can be detected in a number of ways, such as rapid growth of credit, very high price-earnings (P/E) ratios, and very narrow yield spreads between high- and low-quality debt. At the same time, limiting the fallout from a bursting credit bubble is no easy task. Witness the widespread damage to economic and financial participants in the current crisis in spite of the Fed's many valiant efforts.

By guiding monetary policy in a libertarian direction, the Federal Reserve played a central role in creating a financial environment defined by excessive credit growth and unrestrained profit seeking. Major participants came to fear that if they failed to embrace the new world of securitized debt, proxy debt instruments, and quantitative risk analysis, they stood a very good chance of seeing their market shares shrink, their top producers defect, and their profits dwindle.

The problem was made worse, ironically, by the fact that the Fed applied its libertarian approach inconsistently. Rather than pursuing the approach uniformly through all phases of the business cycle, the central bank adhered to its hands-off approach during monetary expansion but abandoned it when constraint was necessary. And that, in turn, projected an unpredictable and inconsistent set of rules of the game.

Developments are now in train that may push our economy in a more socialistic direction, away from economic democracy, whatever its imperfections. Credit crises tend to disenfranchise the middle class, impoverish low-income groups, threaten democratic institutions, and encourage the growth of central government. History has shown that when credit crises are severe enough, they can lead to political realignment or even social upheaval.

These are several of the reasons I recommend that we should fundamentally reexamine the role of the Federal Reserve and the supervision of our financial institutions. Are the current arrangements within the Fed structure adequate—from its regional representation to its compensation for chairman and governors and its terms of office for governors? How can the Fed's decision-making process be improved? What information flow is missing on a timely basis? In essence, if we were to create a new central bank from the ground up today, how would it differ from the incumbent system? At a minimum, the Fed's sensitivity to financial excesses must be improved.

As some readers know, I have long advocated centralized supervision of our financial system. The first time I did so was in a paper I delivered at the Federal Reserve Bank of Kansas City Symposium at Jackson Hotel 25 years ago. At the heart of the oversight issue is how to deal with the huge financial conglomerates that are now recognized as too big to fail. Here are two proposals to consider. One is to require them to spin off assets in their holding company structure, especially those that created conflicts of interest and contributed to excessive practices. The other is to make sure they are too *good* to fail. That will require tight oversight and constraints on their assets and profit growth. They would become financial public utilities.

To oversee these too-big-to-fail institutions, we need a new institution that we can provisionally call the Federal Financial Oversight Authority (FFOA). Among other things, the FFOA would assess capital adequacy, the soundness of trading practices, vulnerability to conflicts of interest, and other measures of stability and competitiveness. It would set guidelines for the participants in the financial derivatives markets, such as limits on the creation of derivatives and the extent to which the issuers of securitized debt (the underwriters) should share the lending risk.

The chairman of the new Oversight Authority should serve as a voting member of the Federal Reserve's Open Market Committee in order to bring to bear on the nation's monetary authorities valuable input about the well-being of our largest financial institutions. This kind of input has been sorely lacking in recent decades. The FFOA chairman, along with the chairman of the Federal Reserve, should be required to co-sign an annual report submitted to Congress on the safety and soundness of the financial institutions under their purview.

At the same time, I strongly oppose the creation of an independent risk regulator. At first blush, this sounds very appealing. But a separate regulator of this sort will fail, chiefly because financial soundness and credit creation are linked. They cannot be separated from the monetary authority that controls the key variable: control over the growth of money and credit.

Because of the thoroughly global nature of today's financial markets, unified international supervision is essential. Therefore, other leading economies throughout the world should be strongly encouraged, as I have advocated for many years, to establish supervisory authorities akin to the FFOA that would cooperate closely with each other.

Of course, a number of countries may not readily agree. If so, we should nevertheless proceed on our own. Some will claim that this will put U.S. financial institutions at a disadvantage because transactions and financing

## Moving Beyond the International Monetary Fund

The IMF has had a tendency to underestimate the financial linkages among countries and regions. Instead, it has gone about its business of fashioning policy conditions to permit emergency lending packages on the same old country-by-country basis, without much regard for feedback effects.

The organizational structure of the various international financial regulatory organizations is out of sync with the new global financial markets. There is a tendency to look at the world through the lens of macroeconomic analysis. This under-estimates both the likelihood of sudden dramatic changes in behavior and the critical importance of maintaining the confidence of financial markets. . . .

Big changes in the structure of official international financial institutions have to be made. Many beyond the U.S. Congress have lost confidence in the IMF and its performance. The Russian debt repudiation set back 16 years of painstaking work toward an orderly approach to sovereign debt problems. Malaysia's imposition of almost 1950s-style exchange controls and capital restrictions is a rebuke of the international financial liberalization of the past two decades. If either or both of these initiatives seem to work and to carry no onerous penalties, they are bound to be imitated in one form or another by a host of other countries. . . .

At present, no official institution is capable of, or responsible for, looking across the world to determine the facts. A new international institution with supervisory and regulatory responsibilities over major financial institutions and markets is essential to limit future excesses. . . .

Except from Henry Kaufman, "A Lack of Leadership," *Financial Times* (London), October 7, 1998.

will move abroad. So be it. American demanders of credit still will be served. In the short run, this approach will lower U.S. financial income. But in the long run, when future credit crises emanate from abroad, American financial institutions once again will be anchors of stability.

The United States, still the world's financial epicenter, stands at a crossroads. We can patch holes in our financial system, or we can undertake fundamental reform. The first approach is politically comfortable, but will do little to prevent turmoil—perhaps even another major collapse—in the near future. If, however, policymakers and regulators, political leaders, managers of major financial firms, and other key players genuinely desire *sustained* economic growth, they will need to take bold action and make difficult choices. They will need to acknowledge how the structure of global financial markets has been transformed in the last generation, and fashion a new regulatory regime to match the new realities. They cannot have both—business as usual and long-term economic health. At the crossroads where we now stand, only the more arduous road will lead to financial reformation.

# Selected Bibliography

Acharya, Viral V., and Matthew Richardson, eds. *Restoring Financial Stability: How to Repair a Failed System*. Hoboken, NJ: John Wiley & Sons, 2009.

Ahamed, Liaquat. *Lords of Finance: The Bankers Who Broke the World*. New York: Penguin Press, 2009.

Altman, Edward, and Arnold Sametz. *Financial Crises*. New York: John Wiley & Sons, 1977.

Berle, Adolf A., and Gardiner C. Means. *The Modern Corporation and Private Property*. New York: Macmillan, 1932.

Bernanke, Benjamin S. "Gradualism." Remarks at an economics luncheon co-sponsored by the Federal Reserve Bank of San Francisco (Seattle Branch) and the University of Washington, Seattle, Washington, May 20, 2004.

Bremner, Robert P. *Chairman of the Fed: William McChesney Martin Jr. and the Creation of the American Financial System*. New Haven, CT: Yale University Press, 2004.

Buiter, Willem. "The Fed's Moral Hazard Maximising Strategy." FT.com/Mavercon, March 6, 2009.

Butler, Eamonn. *Milton Friedman: A Guide to His Economic Thought*. New York: Universe Books, 1985.

Calomiris, Charles. "The Regulatory Record of the Greenspan Fed." *American Economic Review* 96, no. 2 (2006): 170–176.

Centre for the Study of Financial Innovation. *Grumpy Old Bankers: Wisdom from Crises Past*. London: CSFI, 2009.

Cetorelli, Nicola, et al. "Trends in Financial Market Concentration and Their Implications for Market Stability." *FRBNY Economic Policy Review* (March 2007): 22–51.

Chancellor, Edward. *Devil Take the Hindmost*. New York: Farrar, Straus, and Giroux, 1999.

Chandler, Lester V. *America's Greatest Depression, 1929–1941*. New York: Harper & Row, 1970.

Cohen, Benjamin J. *Global Monetary Governance*. London: Routledge, 2008.

Cohen, Benjamin J. *In Whose Interest? International Banking and American Foreign Policy*. New Haven, CT: Yale University Press, 1986.

Corrigan, Gerald. *Large Integrated Financial Intermediaries and the Public Interest*. New York: Goldman Sachs & Co., April 2004.

D'Arista, Jane W. *The Evolution of U.S. Finance*. 2 vols. Armonk, NY: M.E. Sharpe, 1994.

Dowd, Kevin. "Too Big to Fail? Long-Term Capital Management and the Federal Reserve." *Cato Institute Briefing Papers* 52 (September 23, 1999).

Federal Reserve Bank of Kansas City. "Debt, Financial Stability, and Public Policy." A symposium sponsored by the Federal Reserve Bank of Kansas City, Jackson Hole, Wyoming, August 27–29, 1986.

Federal Reserve Bank of Kansas City. "Global Economic Integration: Opportunities and Challenges." A symposium sponsored by the Federal Reserve Bank of Kansas City, Jackson Hole, Wyoming, August 24–26, 2000.

Federal Reserve Bank of Kansas City. "New Challenges for Monetary Policy." A symposium sponsored by the Federal Reserve Bank of Kansas City, Jackson Hole, Wyoming, August 26–28, 1999.

Federal Reserve Bank of Kansas City. "Restructuring the Financial System." A symposium sponsored by the Federal Reserve Bank of Kansas City, Jackson Hole, Wyoming, August 20–22, 1987.

Friedman, Milton and Rose. *Free To Choose: A Personal Statement.* New York: Harcourt Brace Jovanovich, 1980.

Galbraith, John Kenneth. *The Great Crash, 1929.* Boston: Houghton Mifflin, 1962.

Geist, Charles R. *Wall Street: A History.* Rev. ed. New York: Oxford University Press, 2004.

Group of Thirty. "The Structure of Financial Supervision: Approaches and Challenges in a Global Marketplace." Washington, DC: Group of Thirty, 2009.

Group of Thirty Working Group on Financial Reform. "Financial Reform: A Framework for Financial Stability." Washington, DC: Group of Thirty, 2009.

Hickman, W. Braddock. *Corporate Bond Quality and Investor Experience.* Princeton, NJ: Princeton University Press and National Bureau of Economic Research, 1958.

Homer, Sidney, and Richard Sylla. *A History of Interest Rates.* New Brunswick, NJ: Rutgers University Press, 1996.

International Monetary Fund. "Containing Systemic Risks and Restoring Financial Soundness." Washington, DC: IMF, 2008.

Keynes, John Maynard. *The Collected Writings of John Maynard Keynes, Vol. 6: A treatise on Money in Two Volumes: The Applied Theory of Money.* London: MacMillan St. Martin's Press, 1971.

Keynes, John Maynard, ed. *Official Papers of Alfred Marshall.* London: MacMillan and Co., 1926.

Kindleberger, Charles P. *Manias, Panics, and Crashes: A History of Financial Crises.* 4th ed. New York: John Wiley & Sons, 2000.

Lowenstein, Roger. *When Genius Failed: The Rise and Fall of Long-Term Capital Management.* New York: Random House, 2000.

Ludwig, Eugene A. "Lessons from the 2008 Financial Crisis." Washington, DC: Group of Thirty, 2008.

Marshall, Alfred. *Money, Credit, and Commerce.* New York: Augustus M. Kelley, 1960 reprint of 1923 edition.

Marx, Karl, and Frederick Engels. *The Communist Manifesto.* London: Pluto Press, 2008.

McGraw, Thomas K. "In Retrospect: Berle and Means." *Reviews in American History* 18, no. 4 (December 1990): 578–596.

Meltzer, Allan H. *A History of the Federal Reserve.* Vol. 1. Chicago: University of Chicago Press, 2003.

Mill, John Stuart. *The Principles of Political Economy.* London: Parker, 1848, revised 1849, 1852, 1857, 1862, 1865, 1871.

Minsky, Hyman P. *Stabilizing an Unstable Economy.* New York: McGraw-Hill, 2008.

Morris, Charles R. *The Trillion Dollar Meltdown: Easy Money, High Rollers, and the Great Credit Crash.* New York: PublicAffairs, 2008.

Mussa, Michael. "Adam Smith and the Political Economy of a Modern Financial Crisis." *Business Economics* 44, no. 1 (January 2009): 3–16.

Pecora, Ferdinand. *Wall Street Under Oath.* New York: A.M. Kelley, 1968.

Ricardo, David. *Principles of Political Economy and Taxation.* New York: Barnes and Noble Books, 2005.

Santow, Leonard J. *Do They Walk on Water? Federal Reserve Chairmen and the Fed.* Westport, CT: Praeger, 2009.

Smick, David M. *The World Is Curved: Hidden Dangers to the Global Economy.* New York: Portfolio, 2008.

Smith, Adam. *An Inquiry Into the Nature and Causes of the Wealth of Nations.* New York: Modern Library, 1937.

Soros, George. *The New Paradigm for Financial Markets: The Credit Crisis of 2008 and What It Means.* New York: PublicAffairs, 2008.

Steil, Benn, and Manuel Hinds. *Money, Markets, and Sovereignty.* New Haven, CT: Yale University Press, 2009.

Stern, Gary H., and Ron J. Feldman. *Too Big to Fail: The Hazards of Bank Bailouts.* Washington, DC: Brookings Institution Press, 2004.

Taylor, John B. "The Financial Crisis and the Policy Responses: An Empirical Analysis of What Went Wrong." NBER Working Paper 14631, January 2009; version of keynote address delivered at the Bank of Canada.

Wojnilower, Albert M. "To Prevent It Happening Again." *Craig Drill Capital Newsletter,* December 30, 2008.

Wolfson, Martin H. *Financial Crises: Understanding the Postwar U.S. Experience.* 2nd ed. Armonk, NY: M.E. Sharpe, 1994.

Wright, Robert E. *One Nation Under Debt: Hamilton, Jefferson, and the History of What We Owe.* New York: McGraw-Hill, 2008.

# About the Author

Henry Kaufman is president of Henry Kaufman & Company, Inc., a firm established in April 1988 that specializes in economic and financial consulting. For the previous 26 years, he was with Salomon Brothers Inc., where he served as managing director and a member of the executive committee, and headed the firm's four research departments. He was also a vice chairman of the parent company, Salomon Inc. Before joining Salomon Brothers, Dr. Kaufman was in commercial banking and served as an economist at the Federal Reserve Bank of New York.

Dr. Kaufman, who was born in 1927, received a B.A. in economics from New York University in 1948, an M.S. in finance from Columbia University in 1949, and a Ph.D. in banking and finance from New York University Graduate School of Business Administration in 1958. He was awarded an honorary Doctor of Laws degree from New York University in 1982, and honorary Doctor of Humane Letters degrees from Yeshiva University in 1986 and from Trinity College in 2005. Dr. Kaufman's book *On Money and Markets: A Wall Street Memoir* was published in 2000 by McGraw-Hill. In 1987, Dr. Kaufman was awarded the first George S. Eccles Prize for excellence in economic writing from the Columbia Business School for his book *Interest Rates, the Markets, and the New Financial World* (Crown, 1986). He is the recipient of numerous other awards and honors, including the Adam Smith Award (of the National Association for Business Economics) in 2001.

A frequent commentator for major news outlets around the world, Henry Kaufman is a regular contributor to the *Wall Street Journal*, the

*New York Times*, and the *Financial Times* of London, and has delivered hundreds of addresses around the world to leading business and financial groups.

For many years, Dr. Kaufman has served on the Board of Trustees of the Institute of International Education, where he currently is Chairman Emeritus; on the Board of Overseers of the Stern School of Business, New York University, where he is also Chairman Emeritus; and on the boards of leading corporations. He currently serves on the boards of NYU and other institutions of higher learning, and is a major patron of universities and the arts in New York City and Israel.

# Index